PATHWAY TO PEACE AND JOY BEYOND INFERTILITY

....

MARY HAMMELL

New Harbor Press
RAPID CITY, SD

Copyright © 2022 by Mary Hammell.

All rights reserved. No part of this publication may be reproduced, distributed or transmitted in any form or by any means, including photocopying, recording, or other electronic or mechanical methods, without the prior written permission of the publisher, except in the case of brief quotations embodied in critical reviews and certain other noncommercial uses permitted by copyright law. For permission requests, write to the publisher, addressed "Attention: Permissions Coordinator," at the address below.

Hammell/New Harbor Press
1601 Mt, Rushmore Rd, Ste 3288
Rapid City, SD 57701
NewHarborPress.com

Ordering Information:
Quantity sales. Special discounts are available on quantity purchases by corporations, associations, and others. For details, contact the "Special Sales Department" at the address above.

Pathway to Peace and Joy Beyond Infertility
Mary Hammell. -- 1st ed.

ISBN 978-1-63357-435-9

Unless otherwise indicated, all Scripture quotations are taken from the New American Standard Bible®, Copyright © 1960, 1962, 1963, 1968, 1971, 1972, 1973, 1975, 1977, 1995, 2020 by The Lockman Foundation. Used by permission. All rights reserved.

CONTENTS

ACKNOWLEDGMENTS 1

INTRODUCTION 3

CHAPTER ONE: The Agony of Loss 11

CHAPTER TWO: The Void Caused by Disappointment 29

CHAPTER THREE: The Public Experience 49

CHAPTER FOUR: Looking for Answers 67

CHAPTER FIVE: What Does the Bible Say about Disability? 85

CHAPTER SIX: Coming to Terms, Accepting the End of the Pursuit 111

CHAPTER SEVEN: Trusting God with Your Life 125

CHAPTER EIGHT: Is Adoption in the Plan? 145

CHAPTER NINE: Facing the Future 183

CHAPTER TEN: Dancing with Joy to Share 205

BIBLIOGRAPHY 229

APPENDIX 235

ACKNOWLEDGEMENTS

My husband, Steve, has walked hand in hand with me through our life experience of being an infertile couple. He has never wavered in his love for me and has reassured me that we carry the burdens and losses along with the joys and successes of life, together. He reminded me, over and over, that our marriage was perfect, just the way God had designed it. Through the years of writing this book, he was truly patient and supportive as I spent many hours in research, reflection, and writing.

My friend, Dave Jenkins, author, editor, speaker, and Executive Director of Servants of Grace Ministries and podcasts, has spent numerous hours supporting, encouraging, and offering insight and his perspective on preparing a manuscript. When facing discouragement, he kept me focused on the positives with sights on how to move ahead with hope. He, along with his sweet wife, Sarah, believed in the purpose and message of this book. They saw the healing message being presented to comfort, encourage, bring hope, and draw those in similar circumstances to the Healer.

A couple of dear people the Lord sent my way were especially kind to offer their support and encouragement. A cherished sage of the Church and friend, Reverend Dan Sieker, dedicated his valuable time to read, comment, and offer his endorsement of this book. As someone who, along with his wife, had similar circumstances in their married life understood and was a wonderful encouragement to me. It was the Lord's perfect timing to come together with my previous English teacher from high school, Verna Kocken. In conversation, I discovered that we had also shared a similar life experience. I am truly thankful for her desire to read and offer her editing expertise which was invaluable. A renewed friendship was kindled offering a mutual understanding and shared camaraderie.

Every step of the way, throughout my life, the Lord has shown me that regardless of the highs and lows, He is enough. I am thankful for everything but especially for mercy and grace through Jesus Christ, saving me from a life of misdirected goals and purposes. He placed me on the pathway of hope and joy in Him. All true honor and glory belongs to Him!

INTRODUCTION

Looking back over my childbearing years, it seems that infertility was and still is hard to talk about. Some people, with best intentions, gave advice they hoped would be helpful but often was not because infertility is a complex issue with a variety of questions, answers, and emotional effects. The personal nature and complexity of the issue often leave people not knowing what to say to relieve anxiety and grief, offer comfort, or provide encouragement and emotional support. Infertility is a condition that was difficult for me to accept and difficult to bear as I found it is for many women. It's especially difficult when one comes to the end of her childbearing years with few answers, medically or spiritually.

My Personal Experience with Infertility

Over the years of studying infertility and childlessness, it became apparent that there are many other women who have had to walk this painful path. As I discovered through research, it was enlightening that thousands of women have shared this experience with me. I knew some infertile women, but no one I knew ever brought up the subject. Surprisingly, I learned over six million women are diagnosed with infertility conditions every year, and the number is growing and is expected to be up to 7.4 million by 2025.[1] Advancements today have been successful in bringing about conception for some couples. However, many still face failure, as was true when I was in my childbearing years.

The Pain of Childlessness

Consequently, there are many women today and many more women in their midlife through older years that have struggled with the lingering pain of infertility and childlessness all their lives. Even with better conception success today, 10% of infertile women never conceive.[2] This is still a huge number of women left to face a hard reality. It is also difficult for their husbands to understand all the emotional and spiritual ramifications and challenges.

---

[1]. Elizabeth Hervey Stephen and Anjani Chandra, "Updated Projections of Infertility in the United States: 1995–2025," Abstract, July 1, 1998, accessed April 21, 2021, https://doi.org/10.1016/S0015-0282(98)00103-4.
[2]. "Understanding Fertility: The Basics," OASH | Office of Population Affairs, HHS.gov, accessed August 18, 2020, http://www.HHS>OPA>ReproductiveHealth>FactSheets>.

INTRODUCTION

If you have experienced infertility that prevented you from conceiving, or if you have had miscarriages and have never successfully given birth, then we have walked a similar path. Additionally, we have a shared experience and together understand the pain of wanting a biological child but not having that desire fulfilled. It is a journey of emotional ups and downs that only those women and couples understand who have desired motherhood, but have not been able to have their own biological children. Like me, you have felt the disappointment, the frustration, the despair, and the answers to prayer that were not the answers you wanted. I understand you. I desire to give voice to the anguish you feel after it appears all hope is lost. What you hoped your life and family would look like is not what you expected. I get it.

The Hope of Christ

There are books out there that address infertility with happy endings, with the woman eventually conceiving. Those books are helpful for anyone still hoping for conception. I would never want anyone to give up hope if there was a definite chance for conception. But, for those of us facing the reality that it is unlikely or impossible that we will ever conceive, it is time to address the emotional and spiritual issues head-on. There comes a time to face the reality that God has another plan. It is time to answer whatever unresolved questions that can be answered, accept there may not be some answers, walk through the struggles for meaning and purpose, and gain the solace and support that have long been needed. You may have already searched your own Bible, talked to your pastor, Christian counselor, or trusted friend, and are still empty and unable to find someone who understands. Since I have walked this path personally and deeply, recognizing your pain and sorrow, I hope to point you towards answers of hope, faith, and trust.

Even though you may feel alone, you are not. First and foremost, if you are a Christian, the Lord sent you a Comforter. The Holy Spirit is with you in all those dark moments of loneliness and despair, ready to comfort, lift your spirits, and remind you of the promises of God in Scripture. "He Himself has said, 'I will never desert you, nor will I ever forsake you'" (Hebrews 13:5, New American Standard Version). As Psalm 136 repeats, "His lovingkindness is everlasting." Regardless of how things appear, He has you on His mind (Psalm 139:1–6), and He will bring His everlasting plan to pass. "The Lord will accomplish what concerns me; Thy lovingkindness, O Lord, is everlasting . . ." (Psalm 138:8a). God is carrying out His plan through His Son, Jesus Christ. You are a part of His eternal plan. Your life has meaning and purpose today and for the days yet to come. He will walk with you through your suffering and down your healing path.

INTRODUCTION

Others Have Walked a Path of Suffering

Second, there is strength to be found in understanding the path others have walked in the grief of infertility and childlessness. There is camaraderie in realizing that others have had similar feelings of loss and mourning. The path is not easy. It will not be helpful to suppress your thoughts and feelings concerning your loss. They must be worked through with openness and honesty. It may seem easier to ignore our grief, wrap it in a box, and put it on the shelf. However, it is always there waiting to be reopened, and we are reminded in many ways that the box is still sitting on the shelf. You have thought about the grief in the box many times like me. Sometimes, thinking about it was paralyzing. After several years, I knew I had to open the box. It took determination and courage received from years in conversation with the Lord, hearing His Word, and developing a trust in His love for me.

Acceptance of suffering is not easy, and the loss of fertility is a path of suffering. But God has comfort for us in the experience of suffering. We find, as Paul said, "For just as the sufferings of Christ are ours in abundance, so also our comfort is abundant through Christ" (2 Corinthians 1:5). Take the box off the shelf and open it up. There will be pain in reliving the suffering and grief, but it will be a healing experience that cannot destroy you but can only lead you to a more open and deeper walk with the Lord. Will you open the box and build a life based on His promises for a joyful future?

It is not easy to take the box off the shelf and once again acknowledge your loss, the first step in the journey of grief. As you open the first chapter of this book, you will open the box, experiencing your own grief as you experience mine. You will identify with me, facing the anguish of loss and crying out, lamenting to God. He will give you permission to open the box. Others will not. They have expected you to move on, long ago. You have tried and have done a good job of faking it, but you knew you had to take this journey towards hope and healing in your heart. It will be painful and bring tears of sorrow, but He will dry your tears, console you, and draw you closer than ever before to Himself.

You have permission to grieve and never shut the box, again, as you transition through your grief, and it becomes part of who you are and how God plans to form you into the person He has always intended. As you work through each chapter, let Him show you how He has always loved you, has not forgotten you, and will use your experience in a positive way for you and others. You may feel weak, discouraged, depressed, but the Lord will give you His strength. He promises to "give strength to the weary" (Isaiah 40:29). Holding His hand of strength, now turn to the first chapter and begin giving yourself permission to

INTRODUCTION

grieve, understand your grief, and find your healing path.

CHAPTER ONE

THE AGONY OF LOSS

Have you ever been awakened in the middle of the night by tenseness in your stomach, tightness in your throat, and an overall anxious feeling? If so, you may have come to the reality that many women face, the biological clock has run out, and it is now too late. Awareness that something significant, life-changing, undeniably critical has forever vanished as an option in your life has finally sunk into your heart. If you have finally been struck with the reality that bearing a child is impossible or quite improbable, then we have both faced the same horrible truth. Naïve? No.

We saw the handwriting on the wall as we explored, researched, weighed our options many times, agonized over no answers and the answers we didn't want to hear, and believed we had tried everything. And yet, here we are again, breathlessly overcome with the stark reality, knowing it is too late but still agonizing and wondering and beating ourselves up.

Wondering if somehow we could have done something different, made one minor change or choice that could have made all the difference. Could one more step, one more physical and emotional risk, one more financial commitment have made the difference? Why do we keep going over the same painful scenario?

The harsh reality is there is a biological clock, and time has run out. It takes your breath away to wake up and know you cannot turn back the clock, what opportunities that might have been pursued are gone. The path of my life had long ago been determined, but I hadn't been willing to accept it. I was holding out hope even as my body's biological clock was running down.

There is always hope for someone who believes in miracles, and I held hope to the very last possible moment. It did not surprise me, but I was like the frog in a slowly warming pot of water to some extent. But then there was a tightening in my throat, tenseness in my stomach, and pressure in my chest over the reality that the water had boiled and I must, once and for all, face up to and deal with the death of a dream, a child that might have been, that never will be, and the pain of being a woman who will never bear a child. In those times, I cried out, silently, to God with my hand "stretched out." Like the psalmist, "my soul refused to be comforted," and I was "so troubled that I (could not) speak" (Psalm 77:2, 4).

The Agony of Loss

The pain in the heart of an infertile woman never goes away. Even after years of hopes dashed and being way beyond menopause, the pain is still raw. The pain of infertility might be described as an unfulfilled longing, a deep hurt, and the daily reminder of a loss, like someone very close has died that you will miss forever. As the years pass, the missing is still there even though the grief has taken on a different perspective. In describing the grief experience of losing his wife, C.S. Lewis explained, "Grief is like a long valley, a winding valley where any bend may reveal a totally new landscape."[3] Feelings one had thought had been met head-on may emerge again but in a different place, from a different view, and when one is in a different frame of mind.

They can catch you off guard when you least expect it. I have had to learn to deal with this grief. It has been a struggle at times, but the Lord has helped me through reading Scripture and looking at the experience of other women in the same circumstances.

Dashed Expectations

A woman grieving the loss of fertility has had a long history of dashed expectations. From the beginning attempt at conception to the final acceptance of no further hope, most infertile women have gone through numerous cycles, month to month,

---

3. C.S. Lewis, *A Grief Observed* (New York, NY: Bantam Books, 1961), 69.

wondering if their dream would be fulfilled. As each month passes, whether specialized medical interventions have been attempted or not, one's anticipation rises and falls like watching for a cloud to bring rain in a desert or for a letter or message to come from a loved one that never arrives. Each month arrives with new hope, especially when one thinks there is a fresh approach or another answer to unsuccessful conception. Hope is soon dashed, and grief reemerges until anticipation rises again. We know this vicious cycle of ups and downs, which can cause us to experience a form of bondage with our hope so caught up in a desire so real to us but so risky to our emotions and spiritual understanding and strength. Edward T. Welch, renowned biblical counselor, teacher, and author, cautions, "Hope is risky. The more you look forward to something, the greater the chance of being let down. No doubt you have had your hopes rise and fall in your life. We all have, and it always hurts."[4] Welch perceptively draws our attention to the Scripture from Proverbs, "Hope deferred makes the heart sick, but desire fulfilled is a tree of life" (13:12). Our hope has been for something we thought would fulfill all our dreams and was the perfect answer to a perfect life. We have grieved for something we thought we had to have.

---

4. Edward T. Welch, *Depression: A Stubborn Darkness—Light for the Path* (Greensboro, NC: New Growth Press, 2004), 165.

The Agony of Loss

The Random House Dictionary defines *grief* as "keen mental suffering or distress over affliction or loss; sharp sorrow; painful regret."[5] Grief is a disappointment that goes beyond the day-to-day mishaps or misfortunes of life. Grief conjures thoughts of *mental suffering* that is painful, hurtful, and full of disappointment, very similar to death. Dreams that do not come to pass are a form of death, and truly the heart is sick, as real as a loved one dying, albeit in a slow, month-to-month ordeal.

My dream as an infertile woman was for a child that I imagined from month-to-month and year-to-year, a dream which instilled a sense of hope. The sense of hope is similar to spring, when life is new and fresh. In spring, the plants and trees are young and springing forth with vitality and beauty. As spring turns to summer, the plants and trees are in their full strength, full of energy and the hope of bearing much fruit. As fall unfolds, everything begins bringing forth the fruit of the harvest. The harvest normally is abundant unless a tree or plant is not pollinated properly in the spring. Hope then begins to fade and slowly withers and dies away with that particular tree or plant. Winter is coming, and the tree will go dormant, and all that will remain is a barren tree reminding one of what might have been.

---

5. *The Random House Dictionary of the English Language*, s.v. "grief" (New York: Random House, 1968).

Just as with a barren woman as with a barren tree, hope slowly died and became final, and there was only the disappointment and grief of lost fruit. The grief became all too real and brought about a *sharp sorrow* I had to come to terms with. If one does not come to terms with the grief and sorrow, one can become lifeless and without purpose. Welch emphasizes, "To live without hope is to live without a future."[6] Living without hope and meaning may lead to serious depression, a checking-out from life, and further lost dreams.

Infertility and Disability

It was a shock to me when I realized that my infertility was classified as a disability. I had never really thought of it that way, but it made sense to me. It had caused a great loss in my life of an important physical function, reproduction. I began to understand that the pain of infertility was quite similar to what one would imagine with the experience of a physical disability. Never having had a physical disability, I couldn't presume to understand what it would be like when an important ability, such as sight or use of a limb, was missing. However, infertility is like knowing a part of you is missing, and there is often nothing you can do about it.

---

6. Welch, *Depression*, 166.

The Agony of Loss

In that way, infertility is like a disability, especially when all the attempts to address it and fix it have failed. All the avenues of remedy naturally, medically, emotionally, and spiritually, had been tried without results. No amount of prayer had fixed it. No strength of faith had fixed it. No surgery had fixed it. No hormone therapy, diet therapy, or herbal concoctions had fixed it. No prosthesis could fix it. No amount of mental or physical therapy could fix it. My hopes had been dashed. Being a believer in Christ, my hope of eternal life and a final healing in the promise of a glorified body was a sincere promise to hold dear and was certainly a comfort. However, while living here on earth, I knew I had to deal with the pain and suffering of reproductive loss.

In my heart and through all rational reasoning, I knew God is sovereign and chooses to heal or not heal according to His divine will. Miracles really do happen. Women who thought they would never conceive all of a sudden do so with no apparent intervention. Without hope of healing from life-threatening diseases, some people are miraculously healed in a way that even astounds doctors. However, when my healing did not materialize, the anguish of dashed expectations was still very real. Satan has his crosshairs on earthly beings and relishes inflicting physical and emotional pain and suffering. Joni Eareckson Tada, severely paralyzed as a youth in a diving accident, brings much to light concerning Satan, "I believe he views disabilities as his last great stronghold to defame the good character of God. Suffering is that last frontier he exploits to smear God's trustworthiness."[7]

Accepting His sovereign will of living with a disability in my life was a struggle, especially when I believed healing could be the only good outcome in my eyes. I knew the Scriptures and knew I might have to accept that there was a long-term, divine purpose in my life in the mind of God different from what I expected. "'For My thoughts are not your thoughts, neither are your ways My ways,' declares the Lord. 'For as the heavens are higher than the earth, so are My ways higher than your ways, and My thoughts than your thoughts'" (Isaiah 55:8–9). I accepted, in my mind, that God's view was far beyond what I could imagine, but in my heart, I struggled with being imperfect in my eyes. I could not see the bigger picture or find any earthly benefit in being infertile.

"The US Supreme Court held in 1998 that infertility is a disability under the American with Disabilities Act (ADA)."[8] Just like in the case of any disability, I was confronted with a monumental loss which changed my life forever. Some people might wonder

---

7. Joni Eareckson Tada, *A Place of Healing: Wrestling with the Mysteries of Suffering, Pain and God's Sovereignty* (Colorado Springs, CO: David C. Cook, 2010), 30.
8. Saul Spigel, "Infertility—Causes, Treatment, Insurance and Disability Status," OLR Research Report, February 3, 2005, accessed May 4, 2018, http://www.cga.ct.gov/2005/rpt/2005-R-0145.htm.

and sincerely ask, though, "What is so vitally important about having children?" God placed in humans the desire to procreate from the beginning (Genesis 1:28). It is as natural as the desire to eat or breathe. Of course, one can live without children. However, without the experience of giving birth and raising biological children, there is an obvious missing ingredient in the normal cycle of life. Consequently, it's easy for me and many women to feel incomplete and disabled without biological children of our own.

Infertility Similar to Death

While it is difficult to accept, the loss of biological motherhood is a type of death. When one experiences the death of a close loved one, one knows the feeling of great loss, the finality, the "might-have-beens," the questioning, the desire for more time, more closeness, more comfort in just their presence, the familiar voice which is now gone. But nothing can be done to bring them back in this life. All that is left are loving memories and some regrets over how the relationship might have been different and better in some way. One feels the push to move on, but sorrow lingers for a long while and then fades as life requires attention in so many ways. However, one who has had a close relationship never forgets and is daily reminded of the missing felt so deeply.

The loss of biological motherhood is such a terrible loss. One is reminded of a death in numerous ways, especially every time you have an intimate time with your husband, and the hope remains that maybe this time may work. I often wondered what was wrong with my body and questioned what could possibly be the problem. When I went to the doctor for annual exams and had to answer whether I had ever been pregnant, it was a poignant reminder. Observing a pregnant mother, a new mother with a tiny newborn, or pictures of families with sweet children or grandchildren immediately opened up feelings of loss. The loss never left, and more and more it haunted me as I realized the finality that came with the end of my biological options. As I looked back on life from the vantage point of postmenopause years I saw myself as definitely an infertile woman who would always carry that diagnosis. David's expression of sorrow in Psalm 13 is well understood, "How long, O Lord? Wilt Thou forget me forever? How long wilt thou hide Thy face from me? How long shall I take counsel in my soul, having sorrow in my heart all the day?" (13:1–2a). Hope had faded and disappeared. I had to face life with the loss that had come to me.

Women also experience loss with the death of an infant through miscarriage or stillbirth, understanding the finality of the dream of parenting a child. Some parents make an effort to mourn the death of an infant that they have come to love in the womb. Parents name the child, and a special memorial service is conducted along with burial in a special location or formal cemetery. These efforts are all important to the mourning process and comfort the parents whose hope in this little infant has been taken from them. However, Julie Irwin Zimmerman has seen too few of these efforts made or encouraged. "It seems utterly cruel to have the great hopes and dreams that come with pregnancy be followed by the emptiness of miscarriage or stillbirth. It is even harder because, unlike other deaths, the deaths of preborn infants are not routinely acknowledged or grieved."[9]

Even more rarely is the inability to conceive acknowledged as a death that requires mourning. The infertile woman grieves the death of her imagined child month-to-month and year-to-year with no relief or comfort. When the reality of "final death," meaning no ability to have one's own biological child, is recognized, there is no formal mourning or memorial to say goodbye to the child that was her dream. My soul cried out, but few heard my cries. A few extended some empathy and statements of sympathy for the loss, but my soul's burden was quickly forgotten by most of those around me. Most did not recognize my mourning over the loss of a child, not seeing the pain in my melancholy demeanor. The sadness in my soul was disguised so as not to draw attention to and be a downer to others. But it was evident to me and possibly my husband in my lessened affections,

---

9. Julie Irwin Zimmerman, *A Spiritual Companion to Infertility* (Skokie, IL: ACTA Publications, 2009), 93.

my stoic approach to life, in my lower confidence, and the choices I made to try to fill the void. "A joyful heart makes a cheerful face, but when the heart is sad, the spirit is broken" (Proverbs 15:13). I often contrasted times of joy with times of melancholy as the constant sorrow of my soul was ever-present in every aspect of my life.

The melancholy sadness will most likely affect relationships with others, especially with a husband. No one, generally, wants to be around a sad or melancholy person. If the husband is also having difficulty accepting the loss and possibly blaming her, the sadness and lessened self-confidence will even be more pronounced. David expresses well the impact of a sorrowful spirit, "My heart throbs, my strength fails me; and the light of my eyes, even that has gone from me. My loved ones and my friends stand aloof from my plague; and my kinsmen stand afar off" (Psalm 38:10–11). As in the death of one close, an infertile woman, who has finally come to the realization of the death of her dream for a child, will go through a period of mourning and sadness that will impact her entire life and relationships. Fortunately, my husband helped me carry the burden of our loss and accepted that *we* were infertile, not just me. Unfortunately, this is not the case for some women, causing them to be even more alone and in pain.

The Agony of Loss

The Desire to Procreate and Have a Family

All creatures procreate as a matter of instinct. Humans can reason and plan regarding the process, hopefully choosing the most nurturing and God-ordained environment for children. We call this environment *the family*. Without children, one's home can feel like it is not a family.

Jennifer Saake understands the importance of family when she says:

> Any discussion of infertility is incomplete unless we explore the importance of how we define family. A *family* is the most basic group in which people have always lived and it's one of the ways in which we define ourselves and see ourselves in the context of the society around us. If we don't have a family, it is easy to feel lost or alone when surrounded by others who do.[10]

Of course, one is well aware that a family can be defined in various ways in today's culture, including one in which there are no children. However, for many women, the traditional definition of *family* is one in which there are children that you bring

---

10. Jennifer Saake, *Hannah's Hope: Seeking God's Heart in the Midst of Infertility, Miscarriage and Adoption Loss* (Colorado Springs, CO: NavPress, 2005), 25.

into the world through procreation, nurture, raise and send off as a legacy of what you have contributed to the world and generations to come. "A good man leaves an inheritance to his children's children" (Proverbs 13:22). Forming a biological family and providing a legacy is a God-ordained instinct that has no rival in giving one the same satisfaction. I believed, even though I often covered it over emotionally, that not having a family in the traditional, biological sense was a real tragedy, eliminating leaving a biological legacy.

It seems that few people understand or even recognize the loss of the family role of motherhood, especially as a disability. Other mothers may see you as a woman who is not a mother but have difficulty relating to what that means. Rarely did anyone recognize my infertility or bring it up. Even if they did, they certainly didn't dwell on the subject. It can be overlooked as a hidden disability; it is not as obvious as someone with one arm, one leg, blind, or in a wheelchair, but just as real for the infertile woman. It's easy to avoid such a sensitive subject when it's not obvious or even when it is known. Even if some have the desire or ability to understand such a sensitive, heartbreaking situation, most have difficulty knowing what to say.

Most do not want to bring it up or recognize you any differently than any other woman. Many women have had little experience with infertility and do not know how to comfort an infertile woman compassionately. The infertile woman often stands alone among other women with a definite, heartbreaking disability.

Disconnected from the Mother Club

A miscarriage is somewhat easier to talk about than infertility. Sympathy should be extended to a mother who has miscarried. At least, they are referred to as a mother-to-be while carrying the child and after as a mother who lost a child. Compassion, concern, and sympathy can be extended because they are in the "motherhood club," and represent the miscarriage fears of all pregnant women. Courtney Reissig understands the feelings of infertility exclusion. "You may be surrounded by pregnant women, newborn babies, or families with quivers full of children, and your arms ache to be a part of the club. But you're not."[11] The chatter of mothers and mothers-to-be at baby showers make me cringe and just smile and nod. It's like being in a club but not having the premier membership benefits.

There were many things I knew I didn't have in common with other women who are mothers that I felt like they should know. Your disability may be

---

11. Courtney Reissig, "A Barren Woman's Home Is Not Homeless," CBMW.org, March 11, 2015, accessed August 2, 1917, http://cbmw.wpengine.com/public-square/a-barren-womans-home/.

silent and not physically obvious, but it is still clear to you and those who know you, even though they may not acknowledge it. Unless you have been directly involved in raising nieces and nephews, it's difficult to know the intimate details of babycare and all the feelings associated with nursing, caring for physical needs, bathing, dressing, and all points of intricate care that are required. How often did I, an infertile woman, sit among a group of mothers discussing babies and felt alone? You try to participate but know if you say anything it might be wrong or seen as one without firsthand knowledge. It cut to the core when I heard the insensitive or thoughtless statements, "You will understand when you have your own babies" or "If you had children, you would understand the issues and pressures of motherhood."

Numerous things were said that made me, as an infertile woman, want to slink off and hide. Besides, I knew they were right to a certain degree. Even if one is helping raise nieces and nephews, it is not seen as the same. There is a bonding that occurs in the intimate moments of carrying a child in the womb, of nursing and personal care that cannot be replaced in any other relationship, even though most women have a nurturing motherhood instinct. I realized quickly, after shunning-like experiences, that bringing up the subject of one's infertile condition will probably not be met with understanding or an inclusive, welcoming response from other women.

The Agony of Loss

It was difficult to find people to talk with about infertility on a personal basis. You learn to even be afraid to bring it up because experience has taught that the subject will trigger several repetitive questions and advice concerning infertility. Suggestions are often given for healing methods, anywhere from medical to spiritual approaches, and everything in-between. Also, advice is often quickly given for when and how to adopt a child, thought to be the ultimate remedy for the entire problem.

Adoption is often seen as a good substitute or even a way to relieve anxiety and bring about conception, although this has not been proven to be the case but is passed around as an "old wives' remedy." Some suggest that talking with other infertile women who are desperately trying to conceive might be helpful and supportive. All these suggestions are mostly well-meaning, and I heard them all. However, suppose an infertile woman is working through her journey of unsuccessful conceptions. In that case, it might not be a good time to try to share one's experiences and advice, especially when it is likely she has heard it and tried it already. It was not helpful or encouraging for me, over and over, to hear the same advice. It caused me to consider changing the subject quickly or avoiding certain people.

While going through the trials of infertility, women try to fill the void of motherhood in many ways. The effort to fill the void can be difficult. Infertile women often struggle too long with acceptance and often have difficulty finding their God-given purpose. In chapter two, I address this struggle that often causes a roller coaster of emotions and dissatisfaction with life, if handled without biblical guidance.

CHAPTER TWO

THE VOID CAUSED BY DISAPPOINTMENT

There is a void remaining in the life of a woman who is unable to bear a child. The void demands to be filled whether satisfying or not. When it was clear infertility was the diagnosis, I was already several years into a social work career. There was no other choice but to move ahead with advancements, make my career interesting, and contribute fully to the organization where I was employed. I also threw myself into volunteer activities in the community and the church, teaching Sunday school, and organizing food and clothing for the needy.

Eventually, we were able to adopt a little, two-year-old girl which I describe in chapter eight. After taking a few months off from my career to help us adjust, I was soon back to juggling life with a part-time career and mothering a toddler. Even though she was a great gift, filling some of the motherhood void, I found myself still yearning for a biological child. Years into my career, ministry, and doing my best to be a mother were balanced against the desire and dream of a larger family with at least one biological child. Financially, we believed we needed a second income, but even if we could have done without it, I know I would've felt the need to fill the perceived void in my life.

As an infertile woman, I became dissatisfied with not being able to bear a child and add to our family. Consequently, I looked for meaning and purpose in other ministry, service, and career avenues. Some are satisfied with being a wife and homemaker regardless of whether there are children or not. There is nothing wrong with that if it is satisfying to them. However, since motherhood is such a primary function of most women, many like me who cannot bear a child may still find it difficult to find meaning and purpose as a homemaker, even if they add church ministry or community service. Even if one throws oneself into a career and finds it truly rewarding, there is often the ongoing loss and disappointment of an unfulfilled life area of motherhood.

What Is Your Purpose as a Woman?

A huge piece of the disappointment is the inability to pass on genetic heritage. People have a strong desire to pass on genetic heritage, a desire which is difficult to replace. It was always in the back of my mind that I would not be able to pass on the family

The Void Caused by Disappointment

name or a biological heritage in any way. My husband was an only son. It was obvious that for his family, this would be the end of the genetic line. One may leave a great legacy of some great invention or scientific discovery, a legacy of some great charitable or missionary work, or some contribution to their community that has a lasting impact. In many ways, none of these can replace the legacy of passing on a biological, genetic heritage and the family legacies that go with it.

As an infertile woman, I did not even feel like a complete woman. This was haunting me. What am I? You feel like a female eunuch, having been stripped of the biological ability to reproduce. While you're still able to have sexual relations, the joy and expectancy of the God-given, reproductive purpose of it are all gone. Even though one can still enjoy the physical experience, you're left with the feeling of being more of a sexual instrument rather than the precious embodiment of a beautiful extension of the reproductive cycle of mankind. There is fulfillment in pleasing your husband while feeling unfulfilled in what procreation could have meant to him and future generations. "Grandchildren are the crown of old men, and the glory of sons is their fathers" (Proverbs 17:6). You are a woman unable to leave a biological heritage for you or your husband. To me, this was a huge, disappointing void.

As I studied the Bible, the disappointment of not passing on a biological legacy loomed large in my mind. The Bible is replete with the genealogies of God's people. Generations are important to God. Having your genetic lineage come to a standstill or to the end of the genetic road is heart-wrenching. Not being able to see the generations after you and blessing them with a family and spiritual legacy is difficult to accept. Psalm 128:3 is haunting when it is not fulfilled. "Your wife shall be like a fruitful vine, within your house, your children like olive plants around your table." When your table is empty and you and your husband sit alone at every meal, it is a constant reminder of your disappointing, unfulfilled legacy.

Why would I be denied a biological procreation experience which is so natural and so seemingly easy for most people? It feels like a denial. It does feel like being told "no" to something so normal and expected. From the time a woman is aware of her female biology and natural inclinations, she is naturally attracted to motherhood. She expects that someday she will give birth and pass on her and her husband's genes to the next generation. Most women are naturally attracted to babies and baby dolls, copying their mother or other family members in the care of babies. There didn't seem to be any reason I should be denied motherhood. Logically, it seemed that motherhood was a necessary, important, and expected part of life. Consequently, when God said, "No," I was left dumbfounded. However, trusting in God's love and knowing He expects our trust in Him, I wanted to believe He is one who can be trusted.

There must be another answer for the loss of biological motherhood. However, I realized that I might learn the reason for the loss or I may never understand until and if He chooses to reveal it. I got to the point in my life of accepting that there were no answers and no turning back to do it over. I had lost part of me that was very important and nothing would fix it.

Mary Schmal emphasizes how deep this disappointment is. "Disappointment and the prospect of unrealized expectations occur often in life, but never quite to the degree that they do with infertility."[12] You are required to make justifications for the loss and compensate in any way you can, but it seems it is never the way it should have been. Never give birth to a child, never experience what it is like to recognize family resemblances, to know you are biologically connected, and never have a bond with your offspring that is unique from any other relationship.

The age or point one realizes and accepts that they will never give birth varies. Some may accept the realization and quit trying at a very early age.

---

12. Mary Schmal, "As God Wills: Understanding God's Plan for Childless Couples," Christian Life Resources, accessed August 2, 2017, https://christianliferesources.com/2018/05/08/as-god-wills-understanding-gods-plan-for-childless-couples/.

Others will come to the end of biological–medical interventions but continue to hope it will just happen, naturally. Still, others will continue to hope, even beyond menopause, never giving up on the idea of a miraculous event that could bring about pregnancy. I know women who accepted infertility early on and seemed completely satisfied with the outcome and their life. For me, I held out hope to the very last possible moment and beyond, expecting a miracle even past menopause. That may seem silly to some but believing in miracles meant anything was possible. The story of Sarah in Genesis in the Bible was always encouraging and hopeful to me. However, as one ages, the story of Sarah becomes a haunting reminder that it is going to take an absolute miracle for pregnancy to come about as the biological clock slows down and, eventually, completely stops.

    I never imagined it would happen to me. It seemed so unreal that I would never have a baby, as I had always expected I would have a baby. Even when reaching my senior years and accepting that all options were gone, there was still a desire to hold out some hope. I still fantasized about Sarah who had Isaac at ninety years old. I imagined what an earthshaking story it would be for me to be pregnant in my sixties, even after a hysterectomy! I imagined it before the hysterectomy, which did not seem too far-fetched. Still, I believed nothing was impossible for God even

The Void Caused by Disappointment

afterward. But, realistically, I knew in my heart God had said, "No," even though I was still not sure why.

When I was a little girl, I loved my doll babies and played house with my sister and brothers; I was beginning to dream about being a good mother someday. Even with plans to go to college and have a career, I believed there would be a time to take a break and have a baby or become a stay-at-home mom. When thirty began to get closer, I became more anxious to begin motherhood. It was a thrilling day when my husband agreed to begin a family. It had seemed important to become financially stable on one income, have a home and nice cars, and to have a few years of marriage behind us and all the basic foundations in place, first. I thought that after the first month or two of being off birth control, pregnancy would naturally follow.

After six months, I began to worry and started reading literature about conception issues. The *infertility* word had not come to mind or appeared in the realm of consideration. However, after a year or more of reading about possible complications, "infertility" jumped out of the literature like a harbinger of a terrible threat or evil that could not possibly fit into my world. And then began the battle, a battle to save something I never imagined I could lose.

The battle journey began with fertility doctors, medical tests, books, and articles read (all before the Internet), methods tried, personal prayers said, prayers said by others at the altar and in prayer circles, and discussions about how far ethically and spiritually to pursue pregnancy.

When all the tests came back with no answers, I didn't know where to turn. I wracked my brain, trying to figure it out. Was it the ruptured appendix when I was six? Was it too long on birth control? Was it the effect of Agent Orange on my Vietnam combat veteran husband? Was it a chemical imbalance? Was I even ovulating? Was it sin in my life, past or present? Was it not enough faith? (A reason some would offer as an explanation). And, on and on, it went until I exhausted the options. Even after a hysterectomy, I inquired of the doctor whether there was anything noticeable that could give me an answer. I pored over the medical biopsy results, looking for any possible reason. There was nothing conclusive. Finally, I came to the point of realizing and beginning to accept that I was probably never going to know. What difference did it make, anyway? It was done. My life was going to be lived as a biologically childless woman.

Disappointed for My Husband

Being infertile, I couldn't help but feel I denied my husband the joy of seeing his child being born. My husband had to bear the pain of knowing he would not see his biological or personal heritage passed on to a child that looks like him and may have had some of his personality characteristics. Some men

The Void Caused by Disappointment

are more emotionally impacted than others but all must feel a loss to some degree. If you are not able to adopt, a husband does not have the opportunity to share his wisdom, skills, and interests with a child. Men have a special desire to share their wisdom and abilities with a son or daughter and may always feel the loss of not having that special connection. My husband probably expected his "quiver" would be full of the blessing of many children. The thought haunted me, "Will he be ashamed among other men when he cannot speak of his children?" (Psalm 127:5).

Even though the blame wasn't being leveled on me, I still felt primarily responsible for my husband's loss. Husbands, though, can be incredibly supportive of their wives who are struggling with infertility, especially if they accept the situation or work with you to accept it. Jennifer Saake offers some good advice for understanding husbands.

> Oftentimes men deal with their grief, sadness, or helplessness in the only way they know how: through being strong. If we understand this, we will have more appreciation for how God created our husbands, and we will avoid the additional heartache of unrealistic expectations.[13]

---

13. Jennifer Saake, *Hannah's Hope*, 54.

It wasn't that my husband didn't care. He wanted a child, not just for him but for us. However, if it didn't happen, he made it clear that he was satisfied to know we were happy together, regardless of the size or circumstances of our family. Many husbands accept childlessness and are perfectly happy to just be together in marriage, regardless of being childless.

Some husbands may express their loss and frustration openly and cause their wives to feel even more loss and regret. The loss can put destructive pressure on the marriage if the couple is not working through this loss together with understanding and acceptance. Some marriages may require outside counseling just to deal with the stress and pressures of infertility. Once being infertile has become the permanent diagnosis, further counseling and pastoral support may be required to uphold the marriage and assist the couple in moving forward. The spouse seeking solace and fulfillment in another relationship is a real danger that requires deliberate effort to avoid. Accepting God's plan for their family may be a struggle if the couple is not well-grounded in the Word of God and a sincere, active relationship with the Lord.

Will Adopting a Child Fill the Void?

Even if one adopts a baby or child, the loss of motherhood in the natural and intended form is still felt quite strongly. The loss of motherhood bonding that begins in the womb is even present when adopting a newborn. And, as each day goes by before adoption, a larger gap grows between adoptive mother and child in the form of bonding that could have taken place in the months since birth. Each week and month of missed bonding moments have an impact on the mother/child relationship and the emotional adjustment of the child. According to Mary Ostyn, bonding losses can bring about real challenges in the development of the child.

> An adopted child who has moved several times in infancy and childhood, who has experienced the loss of a first parent, or who has spent months or years in an orphanage is likely to have attachment challenges and will need years of steady, patient parenting to become well attached.[14]

Biological bonding can never be replaced. Motherhood bonding with a child may be satisfied to a degree with adoption but never fully met. Much has been missed, already. The bond that would have been formed in the womb and the early nurturing hours while the baby was so dependent on the love and care of its mother is missing. These are bonding

---

14. Mary Ostyn, *Forever Mom: What to Expect When You're Adopting* (Nashville, TN: Thomas Nelson, 2014), 56, Kindle.

feelings that can never be retrieved. The child will suffer this separation from bonding as well as the mother. Suppose one is able to adopt an infant. In that case, there is a greater chance of a healthy bonding. Still, the bond formed in the biological mother's womb with the child is now missing and can cause a severe deficiency in future bonding with the adoptive mother. Consequently, despite the many rewards of raising an adopted child, there will still be a missing element, a void that will never be filled.

Even though it was hard to admit, accepting adoption as an alternative came with some pain, suffering, and disappointment that had been very personal. For the most part, other than with my husband, the emotional struggle had been kept private. It certainly would not have been wise or compassionate to allow our adopted child to feel she had not somehow been good enough to replace the need of a biological child. It would not have been right to speak of the desire for a biological child in front of our adopted child as that would've caused feelings of inadequacy in not being able to fill the void for me as an adoptive mother. Being able to adopt a child was certainly a gift we celebrated, and most adoptive parents would agree but still there was an unavoidable void left unfulfilled.

Through many years and conversations with family and friends, excuses were made and a happy face was put on to disguise the pain and disappointment.

The Void Caused by Disappointment

The fulfilled wife, career woman, and church and community volunteer played the role well with all the rewarding experiences and accolades. Even at a huge baby shower thrown for us and our adopted two-year-old daughter, I put on a happy face but I felt like an imposter. Of course, I was happy to have the great opportunity and gift of raising a beautiful, little girl but deep down, I knew I was her substitute mother, a counterfeit. Even at two, she knew it, and looking back on it, I knew she knew it. She was all smiles and loved her beautiful, new clothes and toys but it was all a shock and an unreal situation to her. For her it must've been like being placed on another planet and trying to fit in. These are some of the feelings that became apparent as an adopted child and adoptive mother began their relationship.

Will a Career Fill the Void?

A career may be fulfilling in many ways, especially if one is working in an area that fits their personality, interests, and is rewarding. As long as one believes that it is acceptable for a woman to work outside the home, there are many opportunities whether with an advanced degree or not. Some of these opportunities may allow a great deal of independence, such as sales and marketing. The Proverbs 31 woman was busy buying fabric, making garments, investing in property, and planting a vineyard (Prov. 31:10-27). The time invested will benefit the home and others and keep one from focusing strictly on the void of children in the home. Having a career was certainly a healthy lifestyle for me as I felt I was a contributing member of society and God's Kingdom. Additionally, even though it was difficult to be around other people talking about their children, I felt I could be a light of Christian love and strength walking through the emotional struggle of infertility.

However, whether it is having a career or doing a lot of volunteer work in the community, do not expect that these will be totally fulfilling. I found that without Christ, nothing could truly fill the childless void in my life. Mary Whelchel Lowman, founder of and speaker on the national radio program, "The Christian Working Woman," has spoken extensively on the experience of Christian women in the workforce and knows from many women how they have tried to fill a void in their life. "If you think a job is going to fulfill you completely, you're in for a big disappointment - it can't and it won't. Nothing on earth can fulfill us completely."[15] If a Christian woman does not let the Lord guide her in filling time with something meaningful, she will become dissatisfied and wonder what the meaning of this life is all about.

There is a strong sense of pressure in society for a woman to have a career outside the home if they are not raising children. There is a pressure felt to

---

15. Judith Briles, Luci Swindol, and Mary Whelchel, *The Workplace: Questions Women Ask* (Portland, OR: Multnomah Books, 1992), 172.

contribute to society since time is not needed to raise children. This is almost an expectation. Suppose, however, the career choice does not personally fit the woman. In that case, if the career choice does not fit the woman personally, it can be a trap and an opening to further disappointment. One could become bitter toward the career since it may appear to be a replacement for a home with children. For a woman who has desired children, a career will be an unlikely replacement. For the most part, my career in social work and ministry was satisfying. However, there were many times when the work was stressful and an inadequate substitute for the life I felt I was missing in being a mother and homemaker. It's easy for a career to become demanding and to slip into financially requiring a second income. Even though we had an adopted child at home, attending a Christian private school, it became difficult to justify being a full-time mother. Eventually, a career can become a poor substitute for a life lived more fully.

Will Disappointment Cause Depression?

There were many times when the disappointment felt like a form of depression. Even without a diagnosis of clinical depression or withdrawal requiring an antidepressant, definite mood swings came from time to time. There were days when being around other people, especially mothers with children, was difficult. Other days, getting motivated to complete a goal or getting excited about my career or life, in general, was difficult. The question of whether there was fulfillment in a life purpose was often the focus of daydreams.

As a believer in Christ, I know our purpose is to glorify God in all things and circumstances, but there can still be a struggle with one's personal calling and meaning in what one is able to contribute. Between the joys of life that are appreciated, the satisfaction in marriage, or the blessing of an adopted child, there were still times of disappointment and unfulfilled goals. There was a definite, purposeful effort put into trying to make childbearing less important in my life so as not to steal the joy of living and appreciating the blessings I did have. But, the disappointment kept returning to haunt and remind me again of the loss.

Trying to relate how the disappointment of infertility feels to someone else is more than difficult. Telling a mother of three children what it feels like not to be able to bear a child is like relating the feeling to a favorite pet. They might have tender and concerned eyes as they sense the soft and deeply moving way the disappointment is expressed but, other than that, there is little recognition of what the word *infertile* means. Only the infertile woman knows that feeling of lying in bed many nights, still awake with that frightening "too late" feeling in the pit of the stomach. It isn't easy to relate that experience

The Void Caused by Disappointment

to someone who has biological children. You try to relate the feeling of missing a vital appointment that cannot be rescheduled causing you to miss out on a great, life-changing opportunity with heartbreaking consequences. But even that analogy doesn't even get close to the depth of the disappointment. Once a woman reaches menopause, this feeling can be overwhelming and can return over and over. As each day passes, it becomes farther and farther from the time of youth when the opportunity was a possibility but now has disappeared. The spring of youth has passed. There is no returning.

No question focusing on the plight of my infertility with its all-consuming disappointment could have been considered self-centered. It was difficult not to be. The disappointed, childless woman has been through it all, crying like Rachel in Genesis, lamenting for a child but yet to be fulfilled. Since disappointment had become a major focus of my life, it wasn't easy to get away from it. "Like a boomerang that always returns, no matter how hard you try, you can't get away from yourself."[16] Edward Welch explains further that there are alternatives, there are choices.

Does one let the disappointment grow into depression? As in any disappointment or state of depression, the woman and couple have choices to make which may, at this point, seem overwhelming but can

---

16. Welch, *Depression*, 55–56.

be faced with the Lord's help and wise counsel. Do not think that you can handle the disappointment on your own or try to downplay it, burying the disappointment in the busyness of life. Joni Eareckson Tada tried every angle to bury or avoid her disappointment.

> First, don't do the extreme of *making light* of your hardship, thinking that it's just a small matter that you can handle by yourself and that you don't need any help, especially God's. Don't be a stoic. Or a martyr. It will only make matters worse. Rather, ask God to show you how you can work together with His Spirit to fulfill His purpose in your life.[17]

The disappointment of being infertile was life-changing for me. Making adjustments to my perspective and filling life with new and different goals with the Lord's guidance was necessary to move forward. I found that the void left by the disappointment could only be filled by beginning to make wise decisions in unity and dependence on the Lord, personally, and as a married couple.

Making adjustments to my perspective of God's plan for me, as a couple and as a family with an

---

17. Tada, *A Place of Healing*, 119.

adopted child, required working through the disappointment and being able to face it while among family, friends, and coworkers. I lived a very public life at work, at church, and with our daughter's activities. Chapter three explores the public experience of my infertility, the many facets of relating to others, and those uncomfortable moments that I had to learn to overcome.

CHAPTER THREE

THE PUBLIC EXPERIENCE

The experiences in public, at work, church, or with family were another story of trying situations and, at times, painful circumstances for me as an infertile woman. It seemed few understood or knew how to interact empathetically with an infertile woman. I sensed the burden was on me, the infertile, childless woman, to react in a way that did not make others uncomfortable. It was a lonely role that needed some understanding to negotiate the daily connections made with others. I felt unprepared for the circumstances that arose, which often caught me off guard, and left me feeling vulnerable and open to pain and isolating behavior.

The month-to-month ordeal of infertility in the privacy of my home, sharing the experience with only my husband was difficult and painful in itself. We had gone through numerous discussions together concerning infertility, the cause, the treatments, in vitro fertilization options, whether to accept being childless and move on with our lives, the possibility of adoption, and much more. Painful disappointments had been faced together as we struggled to find peace with our childless condition. Nothing, however, jolts one out of any peace and acceptance achieved like the public exposure of childlessness among family, friends, work peers, and the church family.

Among the Family

Normally, the family is the first to begin asking questions beginning with parents. Of course, it is somewhat expected as parents are typically anxious for grandkids. If one already has siblings with children this pressure can be somewhat alleviated. If education is still being completed and they're in the beginning stages of an obvious career path, the childless couple can be protected from typical questions like, "When are you going to start your family?" The couple may not even be trying to start a family at this point. However, as the woman grows older and her siblings all have children, the pressure grows stronger to begin a family. Once a couple announces that they are ready and trying to conceive, then all eyes are on them. Everyone in the family waits with anticipation for the new addition to the family. We heard comments about how new little ones would add to "the cousins" as part of the growing clan. And even more stressful, if there are no boys on the husband's

The Public Experience

side of the family, the pressure mounts to produce a male to carry on the family name. My husband is an only son, and even though there was rarely a strong emphasis on a male heir, it was mentioned and recognized. While these pressures may be expressed with kindness and lightheartedness, the expectation of achieving a motherhood role and providing a genetic heir in the family was still there.

As the years went by and it became apparent there was a problem with bearing children, the attitude from family members became even more questioning. "Have you tried 'this' method?" "Have you determined when you ovulate?" "Have you seen a fertility specialist?" "What tests have you had done?" "Have you checked your pH levels?" "Are you taking your vitamins?" "Are you under too much stress?" "Maybe you should take a vacation?" "Read 'this' book." "I know someone who tried 'this' and it worked for them." "Have you tried standing on your head?" On and on, the questions and advice went. Some of it wasn't very comfortable. After a while with such questioning, you tend to avoid family, especially in the company of their children.

As time went on, some of the comments became cruel and hurtful. "You would not understand how to handle this discipline issue since you do not have children?" "You know, the biological clock is ticking?" "You must have plenty of time to do whatever you want with your husband, since you have no children to worry about?" "I guess you haven't quite figured out how it happens." "Just relax, and it will happen." We noticed fewer invitations to family events centered round children, special parties, trips to the park, invitations to babysit, and so on. The intention might have been to shield us from the absence of our children but it also made us feel terribly left out. As Mary Schmal explains, there is a stigma attached to being childless.

> There is an ageless stigma connected to being childless that couples who have been blessed with children need to understand and be sensitive to. Childless couples may feel uncomfortable being with married friends who have children. The subject of children too often dominates conversation. Childless couples cringe at comments such as, 'We're going to wait a year before having our next child.'"[18]

Birth announcements of family and friends are usually a joyful and exciting event for most people. Outwardly, childless women may show great joy and excitement for the mother but inside dwells a longing and a fit of jealousy that is difficult to overcome. With social media and announcement

---

18. Schmal, "As God Wills," accessed August 2, 2017, 2.

The Public Experience

programs, parents can announce the pregnancy with ultrasound pictures and great creativity conjuring up feelings of excitement and praise from all the family and friends. Once the baby arrives, pictures surrounded by adorable frames are disseminated either in the mail or through social media to hundreds of friends and family who respond with loving and joyful comments. Everyone is thrilled except the childless woman who may put on an excited face while still harboring anguish and pain for what they have been denied.

Baby Showers

Baby showers are a special time to bless the mother-to-be and take part in the joy and excitement of the little one soon to be a part of the family. Childless women can only watch with a sense of longing as the mother-to-be, usually far along in her pregnancy, opens each gift while she and the guests all squeal over each outfit or babycare item. The mother-to-be requires special attention as it is difficult for her to move about, and everyone makes sure she is comfortable and receives extra special attention and care. The attention is well-deserved but may cause the childless woman to feel envious of what she never experienced. Jennifer Saake explains her emotions of envy experienced at baby showers,

While I longed to rejoice with those who were rejoicing, my envy was too strong. It was not worth the emotional toll or the spiritual setbacks to continue attending events that only made me focus on what I did not have.[19]

Little did I know that I would look back on the baby showers of our early married years, not realizing that I would never have a baby shower given for me as a pregnant woman. Ironically, I even gave a shower during the first year of our marriage for a friend who went into labor during the shower. She made it to the hospital and delivered her first child. It was an experience that was etched in my brain and added to the baggage of longings in later years.

Envy is a strong emotion that comes with a covetous desire to have what someone else has. It can cause one to be selfish and self-centered, believing you deserve whatever the other person has more than they do. The emotions contained within envy can run the gamut of resentment, bitterness, anger, ridicule, spitefulness, ingratitude, hatefulness, and more. "For we also once were foolish ourselves, disobedient, deceived, enslaved to various lusts and pleasures, spending our life in malice and envy, hateful and hating one another" (Titus 3:3).

---

19. Saake, *Hannah's Hope*, 39.

The Public Experience

Envy says to God, "You do not know what I need or when I need it. I know better than you what is right for me and my life." It is a sin that blinds one from the joys, blessings, and gifts already provided by God. Envy can cause bitterness toward God, thus, diminishing the closeness between the childless woman and God. I would have to admit there were some bitterness mixed with a feeling of rejection. I did not want to have those feelings toward God, blame Him, or be envious of others He had blessed, but these emotions were often difficult to control. The envy was difficult to control during my years of trying to conceive and much later, even after menopause and the obvious end of hope for a biological child. I often had to go back to God and ask, "What are you doing? Why has this happened to me?"

Hospital Nurseries

Nurseries at the hospital are a place where one can easily observe and take part in the joy of a new life. However, for the childless woman, these are places where reality is starkly obvious. Observing your sibling's or friend's newborn at the hospital nursery is a special time. These little ones are precious, but none of them will be one the childless woman can call her own or one with whom she can share an especially close bond.

The maternity ward in the hospital is foreign territory where numerous pregnant women can be heard and seen in the process of childbirth. It certainly was a place I only entered when a sister or close friend had given birth. The sights, sounds, and total environment were strange since I had never experienced being a candidate for this domain. Of course, I was happy for the new mother but felt so out of touch. Understandably, as a childless woman, I had mixed feelings as I was glad, to a certain extent, to not be in their position when I heard their birthing cries, but still envious when hearing and seeing the great reward of their labor.

Baptisms and Dedications

Childless women stand by and watch families experience the baptism or dedication of their babies. Christening gowns and special outfits are often passed down in the family. Little plaster hands or other mementos are created. Comparisons are made to parents, grandparents, and ancestors' baby pictures. The baptism or dedication may be celebrated with a small family gathering or possibly a gala affair with friends and family. The whole family usually turns out for such an affair and the entire congregation rejoices with the parents. Congratulatory comments and toasts are given to the new parents. This is a happy time but also a vulnerable time for the childless couple. Relatives and old family friends often "come out of the woodwork" and soon repeat to the childless couple the same monotonous questions concerning their childbearing plans the immediate family already asked. It can be a very uncomfortable time during a joyful celebration.

Mother's Day

Mother's Day is a special time to honor mothers who have spent endless hours nurturing their children long into adulthood. Women who have not given birth to a child are always empty and find it difficult to take joy in this day when there is a hole in their hearts knowing they will never experience this honor, fully. The church may do its best to offer all the women a carnation or some other token of honor. They may even mention that some women have not given birth but still need to be honored for their nurturing role as a woman. It is kind to make an inclusive gesture toward the childless woman during the church service but the carefully crafted words generally fall short to no one's fault. There is no way to feel fully included.

The family may also have difficulty knowing how to include a childless woman during Mother's Day, especially if the matriarch has passed on. The tendency may be just to ignore childless siblings. Mother's Day and Father's Day can be lonely days for childless couples. It is easy to feel left out.

Certainly, the blessing of having an adopted child made a great deal of difference in that we could claim Mother's Day and Father's Day, legitimately, to a certain extent. Our adopted daughter called me "Mommy," and I felt attached to her in many ways. We tried to believe she was just like our own biological child, but we knew that she wasn't, as the years went by, especially when it became evident that our attempts to bond had fallen short. I knew we were still missing the legitimate claim on Mother's Day and Father's Day.

Social Media

Mothers-to-be have a habit of posting their pregnancy pictures at every stage on social media. The pictures of a pregnant friend or family member showing off their growing tummy are sweet and a joy for those who know and love her. However, these encounters are a constant reminder of what she will never experience for the childless, infertile woman. Even though the childless woman wants to celebrate with the pregnant woman, there is always a tinge of sorrow and regret no matter how well one has accepted and adjusted to the disappointment and loss.

After the baby is born, numerous postings are made of the newborn at each stage of development. I experienced mixed feelings of being happy for the new mother while still feeling envy and sorrow, and longing for that little one that will never be.

The Public Experience

Among Work–Life Peers

Most working environments allow and sometimes encourage lunchtime or after-work gatherings and parties to honor staff for birthdays, retirement send-offs, advancement opportunities, wedding showers, and baby showers. Friendships are often formed in these work settings, which are positive for the company and the staff. If there is an attitude of celebrating family life in the company, invariably, there will be a staff baby shower at lunch or at someone's home after work. Women, especially, are expected to attend. Childless women on the staff will often wonder when it will be their turn for their peers to celebrate with them.

I would often see pictures of family members, including children and grandchildren, on desks, credenzas, taped around computer screens, bulletin boards, and just about anywhere one is regularly working. New pictures of babies and children are often shared readily among the staff, during break, and around the water cooler. These are all wonderful activities, and no one would want it otherwise, but for me, the childless woman, they were filled with emotional, stressful moments that just made me feel more out of sync and left out.

It is common to see a pregnant woman in the office or workplace in today's working world. Many women will work right up until delivery and then take maternity leave to enjoy as much time as possible with their newborn. Comments are made regularly on how things are going with the pregnancy, how their "baby bump" is growing and expressions of excitement are made over their ultrasound pictures as they are being shared with everyone. On a regular basis, tummies are measured and exposed for pictures in tight tops or bare skin. Squeals and laughter are heard as mothers-to-be bring in their latest baby outfits given to them or that they just purchased on their lunch break. Slideshows on their phones of the nursery room at home are shown to all who have any slight interest.

After all the showers, sharing, and pictures, the glorious day finally arrives and it is announced that the mother-to-be is in delivery. Anticipation ramps up. Gender balloons may have already been purchased as the gender is usually already known or soon will be. The desk area of the mother will be decorated with the balloons "It's a Girl" or "It's a Boy" and a picture of the newborn, as soon as it is available. Tales soon begin to pour in from all the ladies who have visited the mother and baby. Things might finally calm down as the mother begins her maternity leave. To top it all off, the mother might bring her baby in for all to see or, when she returns to work, even enroll the baby in the company nursery which has become common with large companies. This is a joyous time and should be celebrated. However, for me enduring

The Public Experience

it repeatedly while my turn never came and my nursery remained empty was heart-wrenching.

Some women are perfectly happy to put off childbearing for several years while they pursue their careers. However, most women eventually want to include children in their lives. Being asked repeatedly by coworkers when one is planning to start a family can be quite irritating. Once the couple is ready to start a family and has no results, it is disheartening. It puts the childless woman in a situation of peer pressure, even in a subtle way around the office, especially when others are having babies. Mary Schmal recognizes that many assumptions can be made about the family goals of a career couple. "Sometimes people even assume that a couple enjoys being childless, especially when both spouses have successful careers. In fact, many would gladly give up a successful career to raise a family."[20] This was so true of me. I enjoyed my career and found satisfaction but would have traded it in a flat minute for the opportunity to give birth to a child.

The childless woman may sometimes wonder what people think when they see their childless marriage. Do they think she has intended to be childless? Maybe they think her career is more important than having a family. A woman might feel guilty for having a career as she might be pressured to think that

---
20. Schmal, "As God Wills," 2.

a woman should devote every day, week, and month to having a family. A career can be fulfilling and give confidence and self-worth but it certainly does not take the place of a family to a lot of women. However, it became easy for me to continue to act like a career was highly important and fulfilling enough to keep the questions regarding children at bay.

Some may think a career is keeping one from having a child. A career can keep a woman from the heartbreaking reminder that she may never be like other women who may be able to say, "I'm pregnant and will be taking time off from my career to raise a family." So, the woman carries on with her career, pretending that it is the fulfillment of her life and she and her husband are happy with their lives and all the benefits of two incomes. Actually, a rewarding career or ministry within an area of a God-given talent or ability may be a real lifesaver for the childless woman. The focus of a career or ministry may alleviate some of the pain and disappointment of unfulfilled motherhood. It can never replace motherhood but can allow a woman to contribute a great deal in her field, which can compensate in some ways for the loss that she feels.

Among the Church Family

Little interest is shown to the barren, childless woman in the church. Some may pray for her, and she might receive prayer from the elders or other

The Public Experience

concerned members, if she requests prayer. However, the number of times prayer is offered often diminishes after a period of no results. After all the encouraging comments about "your prayers will be answered soon" and "the Lord will bring a pregnancy soon," "just have faith," "just relax," there is usually a slowly declining interest and concern. The barren woman becomes an unfortunate woman with whom no one discusses the issue of being childless. There is an attitude of sympathy, but with resignation since it appeared to me that no one knew what to do or say to help and would rather not address the barren, childless woman's pain and loss.

The Christian Church is a stalwart supporter of the sanctity of marriage and in full support of families. Families, for the most part, mean parents with children. Children are portrayed as a blessing from God which they are. "Behold, children are a heritage from the Lord, the fruit of the womb is a reward. Like arrows in the hand of a warrior are the children of one's youth. Blessed is the man who fills his quiver with them" (Psalm 127:3–5 English Standard Version). It is easy for the childless couple in the church to feel like outsiders, given the understandable focus on families with children.

Much church activity is centered round supporting and encouraging families with children. Families with children often spend a great deal of time in these activities and spend time together within and outside the church as they draw close through shared association. We found being without children could easily cause us to be left out of the mix. It is like being in a club but never being asked to participate or be on any committees because you do not have the same experience or things in common with the other members. Even if one is deeply involved in ministry roles in the church, there is still somewhat of a natural exclusion from situations and events geared towards families with children.

In previous generations, not being able to have children was seen as a terrible loss. Unless there was some obvious physical impairment, it had been common to consider childlessness almost as a curse. This is not so much the case today as children are often seen as obstacles to women having a successful career or interference in the couple's plans for travel, business, or other time-consuming activities. However, there is more pressure within the church to "be fruitful and multiply" (Genesis 1:22).

In the past, people often looked for reasons to explain childlessness as possibly from some resistance or lack of faith, especially on the part of the woman. Couples were told they did not have the right type of or enough faith to conceive. Some would even suggest there was an unrepentant sin blocking a pregnancy. After my numerous trips to the altar for prayer and counseling with the pastor and elders, I was still disappointed and made to feel there was a spiritual

The Public Experience

blockage to conception. Fortunately, this attitude is not as pervasive in the church, although one can still feel like a pariah within the church as families with children are honored and nurtured, and rightly so.

Nothing cuts to the bone for the childless woman in the church more than insensitive comments from friends, within or outside the church, who ask why there are no children. The need to explain over and over that one has no children, even though the desire is still there, can be burdening. One person laughed and characterized me, personally, as a "fallow doe." It isn't easy to know how to act at that point. I tried not to look at him or show horror and embarrassment, attempting not to say anything rude or nasty as it was clear he did not understand the loss or pain of not having a child.

Many well-meaning people in and outside the church also have suggestions for how to become pregnant. When suggestions were offered, I had to run down the list, again, of all I had done to achieve pregnancy to satisfy them that there was little more I could do. When they wouldn't back off, I ended up explaining how much had already been done to try to achieve pregnancy and the spiritual and ethical choices which have already been considered. The advice from church friends was often about relaxing and keeping stress low, praying, and addressing any sin issues or lack of faith, the typical health issues, keeping ovulation charts, and on and on.

These are all burdens put primarily on the childless woman. Rarely is the pressure on the husband to do something different to increase the chances of pregnancy. Embarrassing suggestions are given, which can lead to other embarrassing suggestions when tried with no results. The woman bears the brunt of extensive fertility tests and treatments and a hoard of suggestions and books to digest and try to implement. The frustration and disappointment escalate when each of these well-meaning suggestions does not work.

Most people, whether at church, in the workplace, or the family, are well-meaning, wanting the best for the childless couple. They can sense the desperation and may faithfully pray for the couple. Their suggestions of books or old wives' tale methods usually are only to be helpful. However, as the years went by, it became more difficult to reexplain what had not worked. At that point, we would've appreciated understanding and support to accept the path God had chosen for us. How I more consistently began to look to God and accept the life He had chosen for us is the subject of chapter four.

CHAPTER FOUR

LOOKING FOR ANSWERS

When we finally gave up on methods to achieve conception and began to accept the will of God for our life's plan, I felt some relief for myself and my husband, in that we could get on with our lives. However, like many women, it was normal that I still had lingering questions.

Some of the questions may have seemed like distrust in God and others may have even seemed trivial. However, as an infertile woman without answers, I invariably allowed every scenario to run through my mind of what could have prevented me from bearing a child and why it seemed I had been denied this blessing. For instance, why would God deny such a wonderful blessing of a child for a couple who wanted a child? The Bible is full of prayers for children answered by fulfillment. But, why would it seem so easy for many, married or unmarried, to become pregnant? Why do some who do not want children get pregnant easily, and readily have abortions or give them up for adoption? Some do not seem to appreciate the blessing of a child while others cannot find a way to make it happen. All these questions and more are part of the process of accepting and learning to move forward.

As an infertile woman, I asked if being unable to bear a child was some type of punishment. Many situations can feel like punishment and be uncomfortable for the infertile woman/couple. Whether a couple is at home watching television, showing ads and stories involving babies, or out in the community where parks and stores abound with children and babies, they are reminded frequently of their childless status. Children and childbirth are a natural part of God's creation. There is no escape from the reality of life as it goes on in a beautiful cycle, from generation to generation. Whether one is able or not to take part in the cycle of life, it goes on all around us. Facing being childless in a world filled with birth and new life is inevitable.

How each individual works through understanding and dealing with their infertile/childless state will be somewhat different. Each infertile woman has a different personality created by God to be lived out for His glory. Each woman will respond to God and others differently based on their faith, personality, and God-given purpose in life. No one can judge the childless woman by some standard created by someone else. There may be some parts of the process similar for all. Still, each one will walk through the emotional and spiritual journey of being childless in a different way and timing, responding to God's guidance, in a way unique to their relationship. Regardless of the unique, individual walk, the path must be walked, and the journey must be taken. To grow to spiritual maturity, God will lead each woman on a journey to face a childless reality that is God's will for her. There is no running or hiding. There may be some answers but probably very few, in most cases. There will be spiritual and emotional growth but only if the journey is accepted and taken.

Who or What Is to Blame?

Looking for the reasons for infertility can be a lengthy process with many times no definite answers. Was it related to my ruptured appendix when I was six from which I almost died? As I matured, did ovulation ever take place? Was there some type of deformity that blocked conception? Was my chemical balance wrong? Could my pH have been altered to achieve pregnancy? Was my husband not producing enough sperm or was it too slow? Was God actually punishing me for past sins, and on and on?

When unexplained pain and suspicious signs justified a hysterectomy, it seemed like a perfect time to just get some answers to presumed irregularities of the reproductive organs that might have prevented pregnancy. I had questioned doctors over the years for possible answers with no success. Now, as I sat in the surgeon's office discussing the upcoming, planned hysterectomy, I made the plea, "Please examine my female organs or have the pathologist do so, and tell me if you can give me any idea why I have been infertile." I felt silly even bringing up the subject since being over fifty years old it seemed ridiculous that it should even matter. But to me, it did matter a great deal. All the years of wondering why my husband and I could not conceive could possibly be answered through this surgical procedure. We had never wanted to explore the possible reasons surgically. Still, now that it was necessary to discover and remove the origin of my pain and discomfort, I thought it would be worth finding the answer which had been hidden for so many years. Could it actually be the result of a ruptured appendix that may have caused scar tissue around my organs that was now part of the reason for the pain?

After the hysterectomy and the reproductive organs were postoperatively examined, there was hope that the pathologist and doctor might be able to give me some answers. Unfortunately, the pathology report revealed nothing definitive. Instead, there were only vague suggestions but still nothing definite. The report showed a heart-shaped uterus and fibroids but nothing that definitely could be described as a blockage or scar tissue that might prevent conception. It was disappointing to still not have an answer.

Looking for Answers

I had to go on wondering and figure out in the years ahead how to overcome the pain of being unable to give birth to a child and not knowing why.

As an infertile woman with no answers, I was haunted by wondering if I would ever know what had happened and where I could place the blame. I struggled with whether it mattered or not. I found myself, though, mentally recycling my reproductive history. My mind wandered back to the days when we first decided to begin trying to conceive. I pored over in my mind the steps, choices and details, again and again. This was especially true during nights when it was difficult to go to sleep, which led to a tendency to review the day and, eventually, past choices. Nighttime seemed to be a time when all was quiet and the thoughts of my life choices came to my mind easily. Questions regarding whether those choices were correct or what could have happened if I had chosen differently ran through my mind.

During the day, I often found myself daydreaming, again reviewing the same reproductive history thoughts and questions. It often depended on the mood of the day, during some quiet time, or when thoughts were triggered by the reminder of medical tests and doctor visits when hope was still fresh. Just opening my medical records could cause me to, unintentionally, see a medical report or history regarding my infertility and trigger thoughts of choices made. Seeing pictures of happy families with lovely children enjoying themselves also triggered old thoughts and feelings. It was easy to fall into the "what if" cycle and conjure up feelings of regret.

Beyond the medical history, over and over, I would even go back further and question whether I should have gotten married earlier, skipped my college education and early career, or whatever else consumed my youth and delayed starting a family. Whatever the reason for my infertility, it haunted my mind that conception might have been achieved if I had just begun the process of seeking pregnancy at a younger age. In my early twenties, many women I knew had children at a young age and now have numerous grandchildren. I saw their Christmas letters and heard about their big, lovely families. The doubt raced through my mind and I pondered the "what ifs" once again. This was the disappointment I could not escape which was on my mind every day.

As modern science and medicine find methods to treat infertility, one might regret that a treatment was not available when they were being treated. Hopefully, the couple has discussed how far they would go in trying to achieve conception. New approaches and techniques are being developed all the time which may or may not be ethically and morally acceptable to a couple, if it is still possible for them. Exploring the ethical and moral choices is crucial to each couple and should not be taken lightly. One may question their decisions regarding these methods

Looking for Answers

and techniques and may regret not trying one possibility or another. However, there is much to consider in light of the number of embryos that can be created and not brought to development. Thousands of embryos are in frozen states in fertility clinics and await a decision regarding their life. Being a couple who is responsible for these lives could be emotionally challenging in the future when a decision needs to be made regarding these embryos.

Some women may not be dealing with infertility regrets because they have a definite idea of where to place the blame. Some have husbands who had surgery to prevent pregnancies since they had children from a previous marriage. When a reversal is attempted, it sometimes works and sometimes it does not. Sometimes, an accident has occurred that has caused irreparable damage to the reproductive organs. Or, a disease has caused damage or infection leading to severe scarring. There may be a genetic birth defect or ongoing problem with endometriosis or fibroids. There are numerous possibilities that may be pinpointed by a fertility specialist and *sometimes* a fairly definite answer given.[21]

Even if you know what happened, can you accept the reason and accept that there may be nothing more you can do? Either way, whether there is an answer

---

21. "Female Infertility, Causes, Treatment and Prevention," American Pregnancy Association, Updated May 16, 2017, accessed November 1, 2017, https://www.americanpregnancy.org/infertility/female-infertility.

or not, one might ask if there needs to be an answer. Especially when time has passed beyond any possibility of pregnancy, does it really matter what the answer is? The infertile woman may want an answer just to help her feel like she had done all she could do. However, after all the examinations and theories, likely, there will still be no clear answer. She will have to accept that there will not be an answer in this life. And, in the life to come, it will certainly not matter.

How Does the Husband Feel?

When my husband bore some of the burden of infertility without putting all of the blame on me, it was uplifting and comforting. He told me consistently there was a possibility that his exposure to the Agent Orange jungle defoliant may have affected his reproductive fertility. His tests showed some concerns but nothing conclusive. It takes two becoming one to have a successful conception. Since my husband was willing to consider that it might be partially his physical problem or as a combination of the two, it took off some of the pressure of explaining the possibility of being only my fault. Of course, he shared the disappointment when it appeared our future would be void of a biological child. His acceptance and ability to also work through the loss was vital in my adjustment and success in not carrying all the blame.

Looking for Answers

Virility for a man is a very sensitive issue. A man's ego can be severely impacted when he is not able to bring about conception. Being around other men and hearing them brag about their wife's pregnancy, their newborn, or their "quiver being full" of children can cause a childless man to feel defeated and of lesser ability and value. Looking for answers together and accepting the answers together can make a huge difference in the marriage relationship and emotional/spiritual adjustment of both the husband and wife.

How Do You Deal with the Loss?

Women deal with loss differently, depending on their personalities, social and emotional history, and personal relationship with the Lord. You may know other infertile women who seem to deal with it quite well, seemingly, and some who do not, continuing to look for answers, where to place the blame, and emotionally showing great disappointment. Sometimes, how a woman is dealing with infertility is not so obvious. For me, it was not obvious since I covered up the struggle with a career and eventually the adoption of a little girl. This rewarding experience took off the pressure of explaining our family planning. Even though I hid my disappointment, I could relate well with women who were openly struggling with facing a marriage without children of their own biology. Even though I was suffering deep inside, the loss did not mean I was living in a state of numbness and unable to function from day-to-day. However, I've seen some women become extremely distraught and depressed causing destructive suffering in their life and marriage. Others, like me, suffered more quietly and reservedly and tried to make life as happy, positive, and as undamaged as possible but still suffering inside and often feeling very alone.

Some women are able to get on down the road with their careers or businesses, or assist their husband with his. The years slip away and they may agree that a child would not be realistic as part of their lifestyle. I knew women who never liked the idea of childbirth and took precautions or elected to have surgery to eliminate the possibility. Some did not find the perfect spouse until their youthful years had slipped away and then it was more difficult to achieve pregnancy but knew and accepted this reality. Some have come to accept a disability from birth or an accident, have recovered from a disease that has caused infertility, or accepted that their spouse is sterile for some reason. There are many situations and causes that women have had to face. Each brings its own set of experiences and reasons for why they are childless. Thus, they bring varying ways of reacting and responding in accepting and walking through infertility and childlessness.

Regardless of how one deals with the loss of children in the home, there is the tendency for a woman to want to know the reason and where to place the blame rather than not knowing. Not knowing the reason for any loss always leaves one without closure and adds another dimension of accepting and adjusting. It is not impossible to have closure without knowing but one still has to come to terms with eventually accepting the unanswered questions.

Is Childbearing for All Women?

Should an infertile woman carry a burden of self-blame for not being able to bear a child? Should the pressure from some segments of society make an infertile woman feel lesser or scorned because she is not able to bring a child into the world? Women were certainly created for childbearing, physically, mentally, and emotionally. However, men were also created to procreate. Yet, many men do not father children for various reasons, by choice, physical injury or defect, infertility, or unsuccessful marriages or relationships which did not produce a child.

While the man's emotional reaction to infertility or childlessness will not be explored here, it is logical that there may be some serious emotional impacts as well. There is little scorn attached to or pressure put on a man to procreate. Women bear the burden of bringing forth children. It is a sacrificial and blessed task. The burden is felt more by women since it is built into their natures and expected by family, church, and society, in general. Mark Chanski in *Womanly Dominion* describes the position of God and the Bible concerning procreation:

> Now, it's quite obvious that this procreation mandate is of peculiar relevance to womankind. Of course, men must participate. But woman was designated as the partner responsible for giving a special focus to offspring . . . Clearly, God presents to womankind her solemn privilege and responsibility to birth and nurture children as image-bearers who will live their lives to the glory of the Maker.[22]

A *solemn privilege and responsibility* are words that weigh heavily upon an infertile, childless woman. There is obvious pressure and responsibility with this mandate that one can easily see and accept. However, it is also easy for the infertile woman to immediately wonder why she is not fulfilling her God-given responsibility. She wonders if there is another task or purpose for her life and why it couldn't be combined with and added to the responsibility of motherhood. A woman can continue to feel unfulfilled and look for blame when it is obvious that a major role of her life has seemingly been left out.

---

22. Mark Chanski, *Womanly Dominion: More Than a Gentle and Quiet Spirit* (Greenville, SC: Calvary Press, 2008), 33.

Looking for Answers

Is God in Control?

God has a plan for your life is an easy statement to make to a young person. It sounds so encouraging, promising, and exciting. Young people are anxious to find out what might unfold in the years ahead. However, most do not just sit there and wait but move ahead, hoping the choices are the right ones, and trust God that everything will work out well. As they enter into marriage, the thought never crosses their mind that it may be a childless marriage. One assumes a lot and figures that God will take care of the rest if one is a righteous person and makes some pretty decent choices. I would have to say, I assumed a lot. I assumed bearing children, at some point, was a foregone conclusion. But, by assuming, was I really accepting God's control? Was I really willing to accept what He might allow in my life, whether it fit my idea of how things may or may not turn out?

As life and marriage progressed, things happened which were foreseen but also that were unforeseen. It is the unforeseen events and conditions that catch us off guard. If you are a problem solver like me, you want to try to fix, as soon as possible, anything that does not seem to fit your idea of a good plan or outcome. One has to ask if the difficulty is permanent and, if so, how can it be fixed, or how much are you willing to accept in the permanency of the situation? In the case of infertility, it may not be clear how serious or permanent the condition is. When it became obvious there was a problem, I discussed it with my husband, discussed how long to wait before telling anyone, and when and how often we should ask for prayer at the altar. We also discussed when to seek our doctor's advice, when to see a fertility specialist, and then decided how much intervention to undertake. Of course, as time progressed, we believed all along that God would give us answers and pregnancy would eventually be achieved.

As time ran out, I wondered how much God controls, actually? That sounds rather ridiculous because He was and is in control. However, it's easy to assume we're in control of many things since we make decisions daily from the minor to the more complex. I also had to consider how many of those decisions were really my own. Many of us do not recognize God's guiding hand on a day-to-day, hour-by-hour basis, but I've come to realize He is working within the very minutes of our lives. He knew we were going to weigh all the options and He knew what we would decide. We had to face up to the fact that the outcome was what He had always intended, even if it did not fit our idea, at the time. He guided us through the difficulty of accepting and understanding His loving care and wisdom to live out His plan, not ours.

Motherhood seemed so perfect and should fit into my life plan, I thought, somewhere. But, His plan for us to not have a biological child seemed

Looking for Answers

like a punishment. I had to ask, if infertility is not a punishment, then what was God doing and what was His purpose for my life? Being denied a natural reproductive process for which you were physically designed but unable to benefit from seemed like a punishment. Questioning God's decision and plan for my life seemed wrong but, yet, I could not help wondering what He was thinking when I was not allowed to give birth to a child.

When I approached my late twenties and my husband agreed that we should start a family, I took for granted that it would happen, soon. And, then, after months which turned into years, I began to believe God was saying, "No." I felt alone and punished. I even felt punished for all the years I took birth control pills and now I wondered if that caused my infertility. I started the "what if" thinking that maybe I didn't need birth control pills in the first place since I was infertile. I wondered if I had been on the pill too long and my body had forgotten its natural rhythm. Maybe, if I had not taken them at all, I wouldn't have been infertile and consequently missed or destroyed my opportunity. Regardless of the circumstances, I realized waiting for "when it was right" for me and my husband may have eliminated the possibility altogether. Although I didn't know that to be true, it was food for thought which could easily turn into a constant circle of "what if" questions.

It was time to face the fact that whether it appeared I may have contributed to my loss of fertility or not, it was irrelevant, especially when I didn't know for sure what caused it. Beating myself up over a decision made in the past, when it may have had nothing to do with the outcome, was illogical and damaging.

A childless, infertile woman might have a tendency to finally cast the blame on God and be angry with Him for not allowing her to bear a child. She may feel God is being unfair and unjust. If no other reason or person seemed suitable to receive the blame, God was an easy target. If I wasn't in control and He was, then I believed an all-powerful God must intervene and correct this infertile, childless problem. Robert D. Jones explains this thinking process. "We react negatively in our mind, emotions, and will against what we conclude to be evil or unfair. We perceive something or someone to be wrong, and we respond accordingly with our whole being."[23] I had a tendency to question whether God really knew what He was doing in my life. I wondered if God was mad at me or even loved me. My very faith, trust in God, and beliefs about God were tested when I blamed Him and directed my disappointment at Him.

However, I told myself that thousands of men and women live out their lives childless or with no

---

23. Robert D. Jones, *Uprooting Anger: Biblical Help for a Common Problem* (Phillipsburg, NJ: P&R Publishing Company, 2005), 115.

biological child to carry their genetic code. God loves all of them and many accept His guidance, salvation in Jesus Christ, and believe there is a God-ordained plan for their lives. Consequently, I began to think being biologically childless must be part of His plan for them just as bearing children is for others.

    As an infertile woman, I wanted to accept that God loves me, was not punishing me, is sovereign, and has His best interest in mind for me, my marriage, and my future. I knew in my heart that it was not healthy to be trapped in self-pity, blaming myself, my husband, and God. I wanted to move on and finally be free from the torment of doubt, self-torture, and disappointment. As a believer and follower of Christ, I knew I should be eternally grateful and be living in complete joy. However, my adversary, Satan, the enemy of my soul, wanted me to live in defeat and continually plant doubts in my mind that God loves me and wants the best for me. In the end, he wanted to destroy my faith, my joy, and strangle the very life out of me. I knew, in my heart, that turning to God for peace and joy was the only answer that would satisfy my soul. Flip the page over and in chapter five discover what I discovered about disability and suffering in the Bible that helped me understand and accept God's love for me.

CHAPTER FIVE

WHAT DOES THE BIBLE SAY ABOUT DISABILITY?

Physical disability is not a punishment. This is a statement I always wanted to believe but with which I struggled at times. While I might have been tempted to think infertility was a punishment or a sign of unacceptance by God for past sins, this is not the case. In Scripture, we see the lives of many who faithfully served God and faced challenging times and situations.

One of the most well-known examples was in the life of Paul who suffered with a painful condition from which he was not healed. He came to understand his weakness, as not a detriment to his ministry, but as a benefit to his spiritual growth. Paul's condition, not specified, he described as beneficial in controlling his pride, "to keep me from exalting myself." He became "content with weaknesses" as he focused on the strength of Christ for everything he said and did. Paul said, "For power is perfected in weakness" and "When I am weak, then I am strong" (2 Corinthians 12:7–10 and Galatians 4:13–14). His physical weakness, as well as the trials he endured, would work only to aid him in growing deeper in the faith and love of Christ.

Jesus healed many while He was on earth. Jesus demonstrated His healing power when He declared that a man's blindness from birth was not a reflection of his or his parent's spiritual condition. "Jesus answered, 'It was neither that this man sinned, nor his parents; but it was in order that the works of God might be displayed in him'" (John 9:3). He, then, proceeded to heal the man before Him. It would appear that the blind man was born blind so that He would be at the perfect time and place of Jesus' passing, receive healing from Him, and thus carry out a unique purpose in the Lord's ministry to the glory of God.

In Scripture, it is revealed that God created each human for His purpose and His glory. Speaking to Moses, we find in Exodus, "And the Lord said to him, 'Who has made man's mouth? Or who makes him dumb or deaf, or seeing or blind? Is it not I, the Lord?'" (4:11). Yes. Even though death and imperfection entered into the world through the sin of one man, Adam, God is still the Creator of all things (Romans 5:12). All things are for His purpose. "And we know that God causes all things to work together for good to those who love God, to those who are called according to His purpose" (Romans 8:28).

We cannot call anything He created as evil or bad. "For everything created by God is good, and nothing is to be rejected, if it is received with gratitude; for it is sanctified by means of the word of God and prayer" (1 Timothy 4:4–5). The more I applied these Scriptures to myself, the more I accepted my infertility. I also realized that many were not healed in the Bible and are not healed today of various disabilities and conditions. Those who have learned to live with a disability might be surprised to find God using their disability or condition to *display* his work, plan, and purpose (John 9:3).

Infertility Is a Disability

Infertility is the loss of a natural, physical function but, for most people, does not interfere with daily physical activity. However, a loss of any important physical function could be considered a disability. Infertility certainly felt like a disability to me when I had always assumed that childbearing would naturally occur. As stated, "The US Supreme Court held in 1998 that infertility is a disability under the Americans with Disabilities Act (ADA)."[24] However, most insurance plans do not allow for treatment as

---

24. Saul Spigel, "Infertility—Causes, Treatment, Insurance and Disability Status," OLR Research Report, February 3, 2005, Connecticut General Assembly, accessed May 5, 2018, http://www.cga.ct.gov/2005/rpt/2005-R-0145.htm.

infertility is not considered a disability that interferes with daily life activity.

Disabled Not Rejected in the Bible

In Luke, we find Jesus' story of the Parable of the Dinner where a man had his servants invite "the poor and crippled and blind and lame" to the dinner because those who were invited earlier would not come (Luke 14:21). Jesus is referring to the calling of the common Jews, the publicans and sinners, and the Gentiles since the leadership class of the Jews had rejected Him. It is interesting that He should use the terminology of the disabled and poor to describe those who humbly and willingly would come. Jesus had a heart of compassion for those who could understand their need and whom society considered inferior and undeserving of the blessings of God.

The story of Mephibosheth, Saul's grandson, is one of my favorites. It's a story in which the compassion of God is shown to the disabled, in this case through David (2 Samuel 9). David was not afraid to show compassion to Mephibosheth despite the possible threat of a family member of Saul's ascending to the throne in Israel after the Philistines had killed Saul and Jonathan. Because of his love for his friend, Jonathan, Saul's son, David extended the "kindness of God" (2 Samuel 9:3). David made Mephibosheth like one of his family despite him being a direct descendant of Saul and an heir to the throne. He even invited him to eat at his table and restored his grandfather's land to him.

Mephibosheth, who was injured as a baby, was not healed but received the blessings of God through David and became an instrument of healing David's sorrowful heart from the loss of Jonathan. In his disability and weakness, Mephibosheth humbled himself, describing himself as, "a dead dog like me" (2 Samuel 9:8). He knew he was dependent on the hand of God. Mephibosheth fully expected to be executed when David took the throne, as was the custom in many kingdoms. David, a man after God's "own heart" (1 Samuel 13:14), showed humility and kindness to someone weak and disabled, despite Mephibosheth being the grandson of his enemy, Saul, who had desired to kill him. Matthew Henry explains the love and compassion of David and God toward us:

> Now because David was a type of Christ, his Lord and son, his root and offspring, let his kindness to Mephibosheth serve to illustrate the kindness and love of God our Saviour towards fallen man, which yet he was under no obligation to, as David was to Jonathan. Man was convicted of rebellion against God, and, like Saul's house, under a sentence of rejection from him, was not only brought low

and impoverished, but lame and impotent, made so by the fall.[25]

God showed compassion for Mephibosheth just like he does for all those with a disability. God had a great plan for Mephibosheth, not regardless of his disability but because of his disability. His plan and purpose may not be evident or carried out in our timing but will be evident in the fullness of time. Joni Eareckson Tada summarizes her beliefs regarding God's plan for anyone suffering from a weakness or disability saying:

> So I stood firm on Ephesians 1 and other Scriptures that confirm God works everything in accordance with His plan. And that plan often (actually, *most* often) allows for suffering or quadriplegia to continue for good and well-considered reasons that we often can't understand or discern this side of heaven.[26]

David's wife Michal was the only woman specifically described in the Bible as never able to bear children. One might think she was not allowed to bear a child because of her insolence regarding how David

---

25. Matthew Henry, *Commentary on the Whole Bible in One Volume* (Grand Rapids, MI: Zondervan Publishing House, 1961), 339.
26. Tada, *A Place of Healing*, 43.

returned to Jerusalem with the Ark of the Covenant. She and David might not have spent any intimate time together after the Ark incident. She was angry with him over how he celebrated with dancing and utter abandon when the Ark entered Jerusalem. He was unhappy with her because she rejected him. Michal had also been given in marriage to another man, Paltiel, while David was in hiding. Interestingly, she never bore a child with David prior to his hiding and not with Paltiel, either. These circumstances raise the possibility that she was barren due to some physical condition. God can close up a womb if He so chooses but He is also merciful and forgiving. We should not assume that the Scripture in 2 Samuel is connecting her barrenness to her behavior and is a punishment from God (2 Samuel 6:16–23).

The Bible emphasizes being fruitful as in "be fruitful and multiply, and fill the earth" (Genesis 1:28). "Yet nowhere does God condemn a woman because of infertility."[27] We find in the stories of Abraham and Sarah, Jacob and Rebekah, and Elkanah and Hannah, that their husbands loved them despite their temporary infertility and apparently would have continued to be happy, regardless of whether they bore children or not. "Then Elkanah her husband said to her, 'Hannah, why do you weep and why do you not eat and why is your heart sad? Am I not

---

27. Got Questions Ministries, "What Does the Bible Say about Infertility?" Compelling Truth, accessed August 2, 2017, https://www.compellingtruth.org/Bible-infertility.html.

better to you than ten sons?'" (1 Samuel 1:8). This particular Scripture hit home in my heart. My husband had told me many times how much I meant to him, regardless of being infertile and how he was happy, just the two of us.

As I pondered the Scripture and stories about women in the Bible, I came to realize, more and more, that women with biological children and women without were used by God. "God is more concerned with our spiritual heritage than our earthly influence. For many, this includes raising godly children who can go into the world and reach others. For others, it may mean serving God with our whole attention."[28] Sarah, Rebekah, and Hannah continued to yearn for a child and the children they bore had a place in God's eternal plan. However, if they would have remained childless, it would not have meant they had no role in God's plan. There are several women mentioned in the Bible contributing in some substantial way, but Scripture does not indicate them as having children. To name a few, these women include Deborah, Esther, Miriam, Tabitha, Mary and Martha, and Mary Magdalene.

Jesus Understood

Jesus understood the suffering of those with disabilities. He not only saw the suffering of the people

---
28. Got Questions Ministries, "What Does the Bible Say . . . ?"

What Does the Bible Say about Disability?

He reached out to but He experienced it Himself. He was ridiculed, despised, spit on, tortured, and rejected by many. He suffered the physical pain and discomforts of a life without any earthly, material pleasures. His life was one of sacrifice for the eternal purpose of serving His Father in the redemption of mankind. Jesus Christ offered Himself, taking on the flesh of man and all that entailed. Paul tells us that Jesus, willingly, "emptied Himself, taking the form of a bond-servant, and being made in the likeness of men" (Philippians 2:7). He knew it would bring him the experience of pain and sorrow. His purpose in suffering like us and with us was partially to show us that He understood. He bore great suffering and sacrificial death, not only as redemption for our sin but because of His great love for us despite our sin.

We may want to know the reason for our suffering and disability but it may never be clear. According to Ed Welch, "We might uncover some of the reasons for our suffering but we might never find them all. There is a mystery in suffering, just as there is ultimate mystery at the end of all human investigations."[29] It is not a mystery to the One that was the author of creation, though. It was not His plan for us even though He uses it for our good in learning to trust Him, for our growth in learning from our mistakes, and for our total reliance on Him and not our flesh.

---

29. Welch, *Depression*, 43.

Suffering was and will be a regular part of life due to the fall of man. But, God, in His love for us, gave us hope. He sent Jesus to experience suffering for us, to comfort us, and give us hope that in Him we have redemption from sin and suffering. All suffering will one day cease when Jesus returns. Then, there will no longer be a mystery about suffering because we will understand the purpose of it, completely.

    Jesus understands our loss and suffering, even our suffering in the loss of motherhood. Even though the pain is great, it still is not the pain of willingly giving one's life for those whom one loves. We do not deserve this kind of love. Yet He gave up all for mankind in His finished and sufficient work. His hand reaches out to us as He did to Peter and infers, "Trust Me" (Matthew 14:31). You and I may never understand the reason we are experiencing the loss in our lives of biological motherhood. However, I know there is a purpose for everything and everyone. I must focus my attention on the One who knows, understands, and has my life's purpose in His hands. I have to trust that what He has designed for me is far better than what I had in mind. We are reminded in Isaiah 45:9 not to question God's design for our lives. "Will the clay say to the potter, 'What are you doing?'" God's breadth of understanding and scope is far beyond what finite man could possibly comprehend. We only see a minuscule portion in the vapor of our minor lives in a world of millions of people, hundreds

What Does the Bible Say about Disability?

of generations, and a future one cannot even predict to the slightest degree of accuracy. Judging how our suffering, weaknesses, and limitations may be part of His plan is not for us to decide.

Is Healing for Anyone, Today?

Should one accept that healing of a disability or weakness is not for us today or has never been available for anyone beyond the time of the apostles? No. There have been thousands of miracles over the centuries, many well-documented, and many still today. Doctors are posting numerous healings from around the world on World Christian Doctors Network and "newer ones in their journal,"[30] according to Craig S. Keener. Many have experienced or witnessed healings that could not be explained any other way except that the supernatural hand of God had intervened in the natural world. Just because we consider the world advanced scientifically does not mean the supernatural is no longer an explanation for healings that have no other known cause. It still makes all the difference in one's view of the world, whether naturally only or combined with nature and the supernatural. Craig S. Keener believes one's worldview is crucial in forming an opinion regarding the activity in the supernatural.

---

30. Craig S. Keener, *Miracles: The Credibility of the New Testament Accounts* (Grand Rapids, MI: Baker Academic, 2011), 722.

Admittedly, those who are committed to an antisupernatural world view may propose alternate explanations for virtually and purportedly suprahuman phenomenon (certainly the limited sort that appear in the Gospels and Acts) . . . What I do not believe is intellectually legitimate is to simply dismiss on the basis of preexisting assumptions the sincerity of all the millions of persons who claim to have witnessed such phenomena, or to insist that such claims could arise only gradually in legend or through a writer's imagination. Such insistence flies in the face of an extraordinary amount of evidence, denying voluminous and cross-cultural testimony merely on the basis of a dogmatic theory forged in a very different era and context (one dependent, in fact, on a much narrower range of evidence).[31]

I believe in miracles and healing. Hearing about cases of healings can be encouraging and exciting. Regardless, I have to admit, healing does not always happen for each and every one in need of it. Eventually, we are all not healed in the natural and

---

31. Keener, *Miracles*, 763.

What Does the Bible Say about Disability?

experience physical death. Jesus healed thousands but did not heal all wherever He went. In Mark 1, we find Jesus with His disciples, following the healing of Simon's mother-in-law, further healing all who were brought to Him. The next morning, during prayer, Jesus was interrupted by Simon and other disciples, "and said to Him, 'Everyone is looking for You.' And He said to them, 'Let us go somewhere else to the towns nearby, in order that I may preach there also; for that is what I came out for'" (Mark 1:37–38). Jesus' response not only ended His time with the people in that particular area but emphasized that His primary purpose was to "preach" salvation to as many as possible. Everyone was not healed even though Jesus was compassionate with thousands. Keener summarizes some of his thoughts concerning the purpose of miracles, saying:

> They function as promises of a better future, of ideal wholeness, because they reveal the God of the cross, who understands and embraces suffering and can be trusted to be found even there. As signs of kingdom power, however, the miracles foreshadow the hope that lies beyond the cross.[32]

---

32. Keener, *Miracles*, 767.

Being Accused of Lack of Faith or of Sin

Some infertile women have been emotionally damaged by the attitude of others, especially from believers who try to claim that a person's inability to receive healing is from a lack of faith or is some punishment for sin. Zimmerman sees the danger of emotional and spiritual damage, "Some people may raise the idea that not everyone is meant to have children, and that children are a gift from God. This can sound to the infertile couple as though God is punishing them by not bestowing the gift of children."[33]

The belief and attitude that infertility is due to a lack of faith or one's sin was a belief more prevalent in the past, especially with the "name it and claim it" theology and various other healing ministry theologies. My husband and I made numerous trips to the altar for prayer over both of us. We never wanted to give up, but after a while, it became embarrassing as people who had prayed, earnestly believing and claiming healing for us, saw no results.

Since prayer for healing is biblical and desirable for those in need in a church body ministry, it should be embraced with an acceptance of God's sovereign will for each individual. Wayne Grudem gives a clear explanation for what our expectation should be as a result of prayer when he says, "So when we pray it seems right that our first assumption, unless we

---

33. Zimmerman, *A Spiritual Companion to Infertility*, 142–143.

have a specific reason to think otherwise, should be that God would be pleased to heal the person we are praying for—as far as we can tell from Scripture, this is God's revealed will."[34] However, we know His will is sovereign and that illness and death are still part of the Christian life in this world today and will continue until the Kingdom of God is fully realized at Christ's return.

No matter the understanding of God's will and our expectation of healing, putting people and, in this case, the infertile woman under condemnation for not being healed is heaping on guilt and disappointment. The undeserved guilt and disappointment can lead them into depression and anger towards the Church, God, themselves, and life, in general. Grudem warns, "But I do not think that God gives anyone warrant to promise or 'guarantee' healing in this age, for His written Word makes no such guarantee, and our subjective sense of His will is always subject to some degree of uncertainty and some measure of error in this life."[35]

Certainly, there is a great deal of uncertainty and error on our part regarding discernment and wisdom about life and God's far-reaching plan. Joni Eareckson Tada certainly has the right to speak on this subject, having been disabled for more than forty years,

---

34. Wayne Grudem, *Systematic Theology: An Introduction to Biblical Doctrine* (Grand Rapids, MI: Zondervan, 1994), 1,066.
35. Grudem, *Systematic Theology*, 1,067n.

while writing numerous books and ministering to thousands on suffering and disability. She says,

> Here is what I believe: *God reserves the right to heal or not . . . as He sees fit.* There are times when I feel almost sure I know what would be best in a given situation. But the fact is I only know so much, I only understand so much, I only see so much, and I only grasp so much of what I do see.[36]

We cannot begin to assume we understand why some are healed and some are not. Assuming the reason is a lack of faith or sin in a person's life is presumptuous.

Is it Right to be Angry with God?

Whether during childhood or adulthood, when I have experienced correction from others, I may have been tempted to be defensive, angry, become bitter and resentful, and spend a great deal of precious time stewing about the incident and the consequences. In those experiences, I probably dwelt for hours, days, and years, strangling joy out of my life and relationships that could have been lived more productively. If one looks at a disability or loss as a punishment, life can be stalemated to the point of being a destructive

---
36. Tada, *A Place of Healing*, 41.

force for the individual and everyone with whom they have contact. The eyes with which one individual woman sees infertility determines the emotional impact on her, her spouse, and all her circle of family and friends.

Are you bitter and resentful, always feeling deprived of what you thought was best for your life? Are you angry and take it out on your spouse, friends, and family members? Has your bitterness turned to jealousy every time you are around a pregnant woman or a mother with a baby? Are you an older woman now and still carrying bitterness that causes you to be jealous of those who had children and now have numerous grandchildren? Does your jealousy cause you to avoid families with children and children, altogether?

If any or all of those questions fit you, you are not alone. I have been guilty of all these thoughts and emotions. I asked God, "Why?" many times. The tendency of anyone facing a loss, physical weakness, or disease is to ask God, "Why?" Depending on one's relationship with God, questioning may take on different forms and levels of emotional passion. Someone who is a new believer in God and His Son, Jesus Christ, might question God from a limited understanding of Him and His purposes during challenging times. A longtime believer who is well-grounded in the Word of God may still question or wonder what the Lord is doing in various situations, but from a more accepting biblical viewpoint. The atheist or agnostic may not call out to God at all or call out to a God they don't recognize and honor as having any right to determine their life path. From each woman's viewpoint comes a different approach to how she might question God and what level of emotional control she is able to maintain. My foundational faith in God and grounding in His Word are what kept me from falling apart, emotionally, over the many years of struggling with infertility. There was always an acceptance that somehow I knew God still loved me even though I went through periods of questioning and sorrow.

Regardless of our understanding and relationship with God, we may have a natural tendency, at times, to question God out of bitterness and anger. Ed Welch explains our natural tendency toward anger when he says, "If you are a person with a mind and emotions, you will find anger."[37] Whenever a person believes what they see as their personal right to anything, including plans for one's life being altered or interrupted, their attitude is that it is evil or unfair. Robert D. Jones explains that this fact does not make anger "merely a morally neutral emotion. Instead, anger is a function of our judgment. We perceive something or someone to be wrong, and we respond accordingly with our whole being."[38] The

---

37. Welch, *Depression*, 154.
38. Jones, *Uprooting Anger*, 115.

feeling of somehow having the right to be angry can be deceptive and move one into the wrong attitude very quickly. Ed Welch points out, "Anger typically begins in a way that imitates God—it makes judgments about right and wrong. But it can quickly turn into a stance against him. You are angry because your rights and your glory—not God's—have been violated."[39] How we respond to the situations of life with anger towards God or not says a lot about what we know and believe about God.

I had to ask myself, when I was angry, was I not questioning the sovereignty of God and His right to deal with me and our situation as He saw fit? Did I recognize God as holy and without reproach in any matter? If so, I had to heed His words regarding anger. As Ecclesiastes 7:9 states, "Do not be eager in your heart to be angry, for anger resides in the bosom of fools." And, James reminds, "But let everyone be quick to hear, slow to speak and slow to anger; for the anger of man does not achieve the righteousness of God" (James 1:19b–20). Recognizing the sovereignty of God requires one sees Him as just and fair even though it may be difficult for us to see Him that way. According to Jerry Bridges, a holy God cannot be unfair:

> If God is perfectly holy, then we can be confident that His actions toward us

---

39. Welch, *Depression*, 156.

are always perfect and just. We are often tempted to question God's actions and complain that He is unfair in His treatment of us. But it is impossible in the very nature of God that He should ever be unfair. Because He is holy, all His actions are holy.[40]

Fairness and equity are areas in which we all struggle but for which I found answers and solace in the Scripture. In the example of Job's struggle with suffering, I found a deeper personal awareness of God's control in my life in Job's recognition of the sovereignty of God. At the beginning of his suffering with boils, he was accepting and "did not sin with his lips" (Job 2:10). However, after seven days and seven nights in pain, Job begins to question why he was born (Job 3:1–12). He began with accepting the sovereignty of God but, then, questioned God's judgment in bringing him into the world and also why he was suffering (Job 3:20–26). Job received no help from his friends who placed blame on Job. Eventually, God explained His sovereignty and Job confessed his lack of understanding and came to accept God's right to do what He chooses (Job 38–41). "Then Job answered the Lord, and said, 'I know that Thou canst do all things, and that no purpose of Thine can be thwarted. 'Who is this that hides counsel without knowledge?'

---
40. Jerry Bridges, *The Pursuit of Holiness* (Colorado Springs, CO: NavPress, 2006), 11.

'Therefore I have declared that which I did not understand, things too wonderful for me, which I did not know'" (Job 42:1–3).

Any anger and bitterness I had in response to infertility or any condition or situation seen as unfair or unjust, which may have been taken out on myself or on others, was actually an angry attitude against God. Ed Welch points out the actual direction of anger, "To be more specific, anger is between you and God."[41] He will listen to our expressions of sorrow and loss, desiring for us to be open with our thoughts and feelings as He knows what is in our heart already. However, if our expressions of sorrow and loss show a lack of trust and confidence in His wisdom and justice, then, we are walking in a self-centered attitude that desires our control over our own lives.

Our anger is rebellion against God in our hearts, a tantrum over what we want but have not received. Ed Welch helps with understanding our self-centeredness by saying, "With our complaining and grumbling, we have set up an implicit test for God: Will he give us what we want or not? We have made life about us, and when we do, we are doomed to a life of perpetual dissatisfaction."[42] After studying some biblical counseling literature and books about anger,

---

41. Welch, *Depression*, 156.

42. Welch, *Depression*, 161.

I can honestly admit that my lingering struggle with infertility was a self-centered attitude. I spent way too much time on questioning God and living in doubt and mistrust of His reasons and purpose for my life. I could have never been happy until I trusted Him fully with my life and accepted, in gratitude, the beautiful gifts He had given me.

Depression

Depression can be an actual, unfortunate outcome of infertility. It may be masked by the busyness of life and career. Depression can come in many forms when feeling desperate for answers and lapsing into moments of not trusting God. Depression, like anger, is a self-centered condition which is easy to fall into when a serious condition like infertility plagues your life. One can become reclusive, not wanting to be around people, especially mothers with small children or pregnant women. One can also become angry at their infertility dilemma and take out their frustration on others, including their husband.

Some might throw themselves into their career or a hobby to replace the loss, while they try to do an excellent job of masking the pain. It's easy to extoll the virtues of a great career, especially where one is contributing so much to others and the community. You can talk about the great benefits of all your free time you and your husband have, to do with whatever you like. The time you have to travel and enjoy activities together without the burden of little children may seem an envious situation to couples with young children. However, as I can readily attest, career, travel, and free time do not satisfy the hole in your heart left by not being able to bear a child and share your life with that child.

Anger and bitterness can lead to depression. When it became apparent that I was not going to receive what I believed I should have received in this life, my mind, many times, became consumed with self-pity as I was not willing to accept God's plan. The hope for a baby, conceived biologically, had been dashed numerous times and, when all hope was gone, it led to an all-consuming focus on self, self-pity, and a depressed spirit. In this state, I had already decided in my spirit that God had refused to give us something precious and, even though I might deny it, my actual frustration and anger were directed at God. Ed Welch explains it well, "Dashed hopes can lead to frustration with God. Frustration with God leads to self-imposed spiritual isolation or withdrawal, and spiritual isolation leads to self-pity."[43] One cannot worship God with an honest and open heart while harboring frustration and anger. If left to fester long enough, one can sink into a state of depression from which it is difficult to emerge until one recognizes the object of the anger and repents. James makes it

---

43. Welch, *Depression*, 168.

clear that self-focus is not from God, "For where jealousy and selfish ambition exist, there is disorder and every evil thing" (James 3:16).

Yes. I had to come to the point of recognizing that depression and self-focus were a result of anger toward God for not fulfilling my expectations. I realized that I might as well have been saying, "I do not believe that You (God) meant for me to be childless. You somehow made a mistake or You are deliberately denying me the biological gift of giving birth. I do not trust that You made the right decision and I hold that against You. I do not trust that You had another, better plan for my life. I will not accept another plan or be happy or grateful for the blessings I have been given." I had to come to terms with this attitude. Without coming to terms with my self-centeredness and self-pitying attitudes, I realized that I might have allowed myself to sink deeper and deeper into bitterness and despair.

Bitterness and despair are not the outcomes God has planned for His children. His desire is that each of us should come to Him like a child, with an open and trusting heart. When there is pain, sorrow, and even correction for little children, they are easily consoled by a loving father or mother they know has been there for them in love through many hurts, weaknesses, and failures. Children do not hold grudges but trust that a loving father or mother has their best interests in mind. Your heavenly Father is the same, having a special plan for you through your individual weaknesses and imperfections that He uses for your good. Trusting Him is the key to accepting a life of fulfillment and joy.

Coming to the point of trust required making some decisions of acceptance and grieving the loss, once and for all. How I was able to accept infertility and grieve with God's help is the subject of chapter six. Turn the page and come along with me in how I truly began to climb out of my self-centered sorrow.

CHAPTER SIX

COMING TO TERMS, ACCEPTING THE END OF THE PURSUIT

The time comes when an infertile woman, independently or with her husband, is faced with the decision of when to trust God and accept that she will not be bearing a child. The time can come at a relatively young age for some, later as menopause draws near for others, and for some, not until the need for a hysterectomy makes the decision for them. Since I believe in miracles, holding out to the very end did not seem to me unreasonable or inappropriate, even though it looked like, in the natural, it was physically unlikely. Letting go is an individual decision and may be a long-term process that takes years. Even well past menopause, the acceptance of infertility was a struggle for me because the reality and finality of it all took time to sink in, emotionally and spiritually.

Coming to terms with the end of the pursuit of conception was still a process which, periodically, plunged me into "why" questions. When it became clear that there was not going to be a biological child, I was often tempted to examine and reexamine the possibilities of physical, emotional, and even spiritual reasons why pregnancy had not been successful. I went over my medical records again and again, looking for signs. I had a tendency to try to replay every opinion and statement of my doctors, review articles I had read that had possible hints, and stories about other people's ideas or similar circumstances. I, also, reread Bible passages that might pertain to infertility, all in a quest for answers. Most of the suggested answers did not even apply to my personal condition, as I found the circumstances are often varied and different for each woman. Many women receive no absolute answer or conclusion for their infertility. At some point, after endless questioning and pondering with no definitive answers, I had to move beyond the "whys" and begin to trust God. I had to begin to accept that only my Father God knows, but loves me, had a good reason for me not to know, and still and always has had a beautiful plan for my life.

Are You Ready to Move On?

The decision to quit pursuing pregnancy was made by me and with my husband. By this time, we had already answered a lot of questions and considered many infertility treatments with prayerful and ethical consideration throughout a plethora of medical guidance. Advanced reproductive technology held tempting choices but these were expensive, challenging ethically, and guaranteed nothing. Reading and listening to the experiences and choices of others helped somewhat, but only as far as what could be compared to our personal life. Self-examination regarding what we believed about life beginning at conception, the saving and destruction of life, God's creative rights, and just the stress and strain we had been through trying to achieve a pregnancy, had consumed many conversations and weighed heavily on us. Along with these, we had considered and experienced for ourselves the financial stress which can easily go beyond what most people can afford. We had to set a limit, not only emotionally and ethically, but also financially, deciding we did not want to take on major debt with no guarantees. Each treatment intervention had required close consideration in every aspect of how it would impact our lives and what we believed. We had determined when to stop, accept a finality to medical interventions, let go, and just let life take its course.

Looking at Ethical Considerations More Closely

If you have not made a final decision and are still looking at your options, it is likely the serious ethical considerations surrounding fertility treatments will be raised and should be carefully contemplated. Each couple must decide for themselves what is right for their reproductive life in the way of medical interventions, seeking God for His perfect plan, with trust and thanksgiving for whatever the outcome may be.

Technological advances and medical therapy have made more options available which may be viable for achieving a pregnancy. However, not all of the options available are advisable or ethical. For instance, for a pro-life couple, serious consideration should be given to whether in vitro fertilization (IVF) techniques are an option since they can result in more than one ovum being fertilized. An attempt to fertilize just one ovum decreases the potential success rate. Consequently, the decision must be made; If there is more than one fertilized ovum, how many will be transferred to the womb? What will become of those fertilized eggs which are not transferred? If one believes life begins at conception, then, discarding, freezing, or donating fertilized eggs for research becomes a seriously ethical and spiritual dilemma. There are thousands of frozen embryos already in storage. What will become of those embryos? If there is no definite plan for each of them, then, it is possible they will become future abortions, if too many are transferred successfully to the womb and a multiple pregnancy is not feasible. They could also be allowed to die in storage or become research subjects. None of these are good outcomes for a pro-life and Christian couple. If you are still considering IVF methods as your last option, you may want to research them thoroughly as far as the procedural steps taken, the current medical science, and the ethical considerations. An excellent resource to consider reading is *Body & Soul* by J.P. Moreland and Scott B. Rae for their thorough discussion of ethical and moral considerations concerning fetal research and reproductive technologies. (See the appendix for details.)

IVF procedures, fertility drugs, and invasive surgical examination and treatment are expensive interventions. Some couples spend thousands of dollars to still be disappointed. Most insurance companies do not pay or pay very little for fertility treatments. Each couple should consider their resources and not only determine which procedures to pursue but to what level of expense they are willing and able to accept. The joy of having a biological child in one's home seems well worth any expense, but the stress of the financial commitment and struggle may reach a point where it threatens the marriage. One has to also ask themselves whether the methods used in the pursuit are an attempt to move the hand of God through trying all options regardless of the financial burden. We had to ask, "Is this the proper way to trust and respond to God's plan for our lives?" God is able to bring about His plan without the use of our finances.

The Stress of the Decision

One of the major considerations for us was the stress and emotional trauma that was being heaped on by the continual attempts to achieve pregnancy, only to be disappointed time and time again. I had to ask myself, "How long can I emotionally sustain the process, putting a huge area of my life in limbo, while becoming numb to numerous daily successes and joys of life?" And, there is numbness to the joys of life because every day one's focus is consumed with a constant awareness of the failure to achieve pregnancy. The ever-present reality is that the biological clock keeps moving with aging and the possibility of becoming successful with conception becomes less and less. The thought entered my mind daily of what it must be like to hear, "You're pregnant!" Yet, I had to ask, "How long was I going to put myself through this thought process, at the same time, questioning what my life was all about, and what was God's plan for my life?"

The emotional stress is primarily on the woman. How many months can one come to the time to begin the menstrual cycle, hoping you will not begin, but being disappointed month after month? Each time you are late is another moment of excitement and anticipation that this may be the time, only to find out you are wrong. Even when one reaches the time of peri-menopause and begins missing cycles, the hope can emerge that you may possibly be pregnant.

Coming to Terms, Accepting the End of the Pursuit

However, disappointment soon comes again and again until the cycles finally end, altogether, hot flashes begin, and your doctor informs you that this is definitely menopause. The reality begins to hit you that the end has come to your dream of giving birth to a child.

I was beginning to realize that there could have been much less stress weighing me down if I would have accepted infertility at a younger age. Sometimes we are slow to accept God's plan for our life. This slowness to accept causes burden and stress as we seek to find answers, remedies, and do things our way. In the pursuit to control my own destiny, I might have been missing great opportunities that He wanted me to realize much sooner and, thus, relieve myself of a lot of stress and disappointment.

Time spent pursuing pregnancy can distract us from other areas where God would like us to place our emphasis, spending time in relationship with Him, and receiving His guidance. Also, our distracted minds can cause us to miss out on the daily joys of life, appreciating the beauty of His creation, or developing talents that He has given us. Ask yourself if you have already devoted enough time in pursuing pregnancy. If one does not set a time limit, life will pass by while being consumed with this one focus. If you have not already done so, discuss the time factor with your spouse and come to an agreement together on the length of the pursuit. Discuss, prayerfully, what opportunities in church, volunteerism, career, education, home, recreation, and personal life God may have. Begin to focus on those opportunities, balancing your pregnancy pursuit so life is not consumed with one focus. As you reach a determined time to slow down or stop seeking pregnancy, life will already be full of other meaningful activities which are fulfilling, rewarding, and already part of the process of living out God's perfect plan.

The Emotional Struggle

The struggle of accepting that one will not bear a child is not easy. It involves a range of emotions. The emotions may include ones of rejection, regret, anger, loneliness, failure, envy, loss of purpose, feelings of inadequacy, lack of wholeness, weakness, and imperfection. As I faced each of these emotions, emotionally and spiritually, there was a desire to deal with the hurt the best I could and just move on. On the other hand, there was a tendency to still linger with the emotions every day. I was reminded that the Lord understands pain and sorrow. He experienced it firsthand for us. Paul expressed his desire for the Ephesians and for us "to know the love of Christ which surpasses knowledge, that you may be filled up to all the fullness of God" (3:19). Knowing the love of Christ far exceeds my personal emotions. In the Scripture, I found consolation and encouragement in knowing I could understand the love of Christ, and it would fill me with all I needed in God, while also knowing my grief did not go unnoticed.

God knew my ongoing plight to bear a child and He knows yours. When month-to-month, year-to-year, I had anticipated the possibility of pregnancy, there had always been a certain held out hope that, at times, make it difficult to move on. Even with medical intervention eliminated as a possible means, I still found myself looking for new answers, tuning in on new developments, praying for a miracle, and reviewing the "what ifs," wondering what had been the block or condition which had prevented pregnancy.

But once the realization really sunk in that there was not going to be a pregnancy, there was also a certain amount of relief in beginning the acceptance process. To begin with, though, the first phase was the grief that comes, similar to the loss of anyone close, or a miscarriage, or loss of a child. This loss will vary from person to person depending on their emotional state, depth of their desire to have children, and the extent to which they have become accustomed to other fulfilling activities of life.

Grief for the infertile woman is not only the loss of an honored roll in life but also the loss of what might have been. One can only wonder what the child might have looked like or what would have been their unique personality. There is a special bonding of mother and child that will never be felt which, although beautiful in its own way, cannot be replaced even by adoption. The bonding that takes place between a mother and a child in the womb, through nursing and care required in the early years of life, is unique and incomparable. The grieving process is part of learning to accept this loss which is very real. Nancy Guthrie worked through a time of grief twice, losing two babies to Zellweger syndrome. She gave herself permission to cry and let the tears flow. "But when you've lost something or someone who is valuable to you, when you have been forced to let go of a dream or live within a nightmare—that is something to be sad about. So let yourself be sad."[44]

As an infertile woman, I was reminded of this loss of biological bonding every time I saw a pregnant woman, a mother with a new baby, or little ones in a mother's care. I was reminded of this loss every Mother's Day and every time mothers were glorified in print, in movies, in drama, and in daily life. Even though one wants the role of mothers to be glorified and cherished, one has to get to the place of accepting this honor for others with joy while still feeling the sting of loss. Solomon saw wisdom and value in a sense of mourning while still having joy in the heart. "Sorrow is better than laughter, for when a face is sad a heart may be happy. The mind of the wise is in the house of mourning, while the mind of fools is in the house of pleasure" (Ecclesiastes 7:3–4). There

---

44. Nancy Guthrie, *The One Year Book of Hope* (Carol Stream, IL: Tyndale Momentum, 2005), 3.

Coming to Terms, Accepting the End of the Pursuit

is a need for a depth of acceptance in understanding loss in life, experiencing loss, while also knowing and accepting that life is not all about pleasure and laughter.

Once the initial process of grieving had begun, there was a sense of relief. I had to come to terms with the loss and become open to what may be next in life. Grieving is a process that can go on for some time, will always be there with a deep loss, but can become less and less as one begins to allow God to fill one's life. I began, with the help of the Lord, to look at where the Lord was leading me into His specific plan. There can be a certain joy in beginning to recognize that there has always been a plan that has been in progress with more to come. It can be like opening a new, special gift and anticipating what special thing might be there to enjoy. The Lord understands the loss of biological motherhood is a deep loss, but He promises to give us just what He has especially for us which will fill our lives with the joy only He can bring. I had to claim the promise of the Lord for me in Jeremiah 29:11, "'For I know the plans that I have for you,' declares the Lord, 'plans for welfare and not for calamity to give you a future and a hope.'"

It may appear you have been given a raw deal, have been passed over, not chosen for the team. All of those descriptions came to mind when I realized the desire of my heart, what would seem an easy dream to deliver, had been denied. I felt the awards had been given out and I was standing with nothing and everyone just walked away and left me standing there alone. I went through all those emotions. For days, months, years, I had difficulty knowing what was next and where to turn.

Joy and trust in God began to grow when I realized that He had other gifts. Children are not the only gift God has to give His people. There are many wonderful gifts which He desires to give with compassion, love, and purpose. His divine purpose for your life can take many forms which can be a blessing to you and to those with whom you touch. It may seem difficult to figure out what other gifts He may have and which one or ones are designed for you.

First of all, I began with discovering who God is and all I could about His universal plan. As I did, I saw myself in His plan and realized that He knows who I am and has a plan for how I fit in. More than anything, I grasped His desire to have a relationship with me whereby He can show His love and compassion for me and receive my love and worship. I studied Scripture with new eyes that saw the plan of redemption through Jesus Christ for me, individually, as well as all mankind. I began to walk more closely with Him and learned how I could walk in His grace and share His love with others. As I walked with Him, He took away my pain, grief, and bitterness as He softened my heart to receive more and more each day. His compassion showed me He had not forgotten nor forsaken me. I realized He had gifts of joy and peace and guided me by His Holy Spirit to share in His plan in ways I could not imagine. Studying 1 Corinthians 12 opened my eyes to gifts and ministries for the glory of God which could be used in my life according to His plan.

The loss of bearing a child will always be a mystery for me and could have been a gaping wound for the rest of my life as it can be for many. Many of those suffering the loss of motherhood will see it as a wound from which they will never recover. I understand that the loss will always be the "elephant in the room" which appears very distinctly and directly at times and other times, more subtly. The loss can be a defining condition in one's life which can control many thoughts and decisions. However, the Lord showed me how to not let the loss of motherhood stand between me and what beautiful plan God had for me. As I began to accept infertility and the inability to bear a child, I opened my heart to trusting God's plan for my future. I looked to the future with joy knowing God had already given me His most special gift in His Son to redeem me from a life separated from God. There was much to live for with joy and anticipation, striving to be thankful and grateful for each tremendous blessing in my life. My heart grew in joy as I took His hand in trust and acceptance.

Acceptance grew into more trust of God's perfect plan for my life. In chapter seven, you will discover how trust was nurtured and grew as I moved forward and began the process of not looking back but looking forward to a new outlook on life.

CHAPTER SEVEN

TRUSTING GOD WITH YOUR LIFE

Trusting God in the midst of your infertility is definitely a step in the right direction. However, trusting God is a daily decision when trying to work through such a monumental loss in one's life. In the day-to-day battle to move on, emotional struggles brought feelings of guilt and failure for me. It became obvious that I was having difficulty trusting God in the painful moments. I knew God, in His sovereign will, had allowed me to be infertile, yet it was difficult in that I couldn't help thinking that maybe he had had better options in mind for me. If it weren't for a fallen world, no one would have to face such a diagnosis. Finally accepting and letting go of my desire and need for a biological child, regardless of the reason, and accepting that God would fill my life with all that I needed, was a huge step. There was freedom in finally realizing that God and His plan were perfect and enough.

Until I arrived at this point and began the path down this new road, I was not able to discover all that God had for me.

Would I still wonder what it would have been like if I had been able to bear a child? Would I wonder what the childbirth experience would have been like for me? Would I still always wonder what our babies would have looked like, what experiences of raising them would have been like? Yes, absolutely! These thoughts went through my mind from time to time but lessened as I began to embrace a new path and life. Would I be able to eventually appreciate the sight of a family with children or a newborn in the arms of their mother without feeling jealous or rejected? Would I be able to rejoice with a pregnant woman and attend her baby shower with joy in anticipation of the child to be born? Would I be able to bless a pregnant woman with heartfelt gifts for their baby? Would I be able to participate in pro-life events and rejoice in babies women have given life? Yes. It became clear to me that when one embraces a path that God has especially for them, they will be able to embrace what God has chosen for others, fully and completely. Yet, I still struggled.

God does everything well. Christians believe in the sovereign, creative, powerful, and perfect glory of God and understand this statement. Then, why did I doubt God when faced with a weakness or disability like infertility? Was God not in control? Does

He not cause and allow rain to fall on the righteous and unrighteous? Yes, He does. I doubted because I did not want to accept the way I was made or the circumstances that came my way. I fought against it and tried to change myself and circumstances to fit my own idea of perfection while not allowing myself to see the big picture of how God uses different people and situations for His glory.

God was fully aware of my birth, physical makeup, my potential, circumstances, and what I would have to face in life, including infertility. If I had tried to understand the big picture from God's perspective, how could I have questioned the fact that each part of me and my circumstances were perfectly aligned in God's plan? His plan for my life involved more than just me, personally, but also how I fit into the entire big picture of God's plan for mankind.

Each of us is placed in a circle of family, friends, neighbors, and community that is impacted by who we are, what we stand for, and how we move through God's plan for our life. What we think and believe impact those around us in ways that ripple throughout eternity. How we accept or not accept God's plan for our life impacts the big picture in the world and time in which we were placed. Robert D. Jones explains that moving "from ignorance to an awareness of God's sovereignty signals progress." As we grow in understanding, we realize, as he says, "God is the ultimate cause of every hardship and that he uses every trial for the good purpose of making us like Jesus Christ (Genesis 50:20; Job 1–2, 38–42; Romans 8:28–29)."[45]

Trusting God with His plan can make a huge difference in our personal life and our spouse, family members, and friends. Helping them understand that being infertile may be a perfect plan for some people, will help them trust God for however He is working in their life. We can help others see that God knows and understands our painful situation or loss and, therefore, also their painful situation or loss. As Elizabeth George compassionately expresses,

> If there are no children, God knows that, too, and He knows His purpose in it, as well as our suffering if we desire children. The challenges we face are known to Him. In fact, He knows—and has known since the beginning of time—exactly how He would use them to draw us closer to Him and to make us more like Christ.[46]

How each of us deals with the "if onlys" and "what ifs" is an incredible testimony when we accept God's plan. Everyone has something in their life they would have liked to have changed or wished

---

45. Jones, *Uprooting Anger*, 121.
46. Elizabeth George, *Loving God with All Your Mind* (Eugene, OR: Harvest House Publishers, 1994), 262–263.

had been different. Some are more monumental than others, some are tragic, and some are just painful issues one carries throughout life. How each of us allows God to teach, refine, comfort, and groom us into His perfect will is not only crucial for us but for everyone we touch.

God Helped Me Bear the Burden

Everyone in this life has a burden to bear. Few get through life without pain or sorrow. But, the Lord reminds us that His healing and comforting balm compassionately covers our hurts and losses as we go through this life. However, we are still expected to bear some pain and experience loss and its consequences but with Him beside us and strengthening us. "The Lord is my strength and my shield; My heart trusts in Him, and I am helped" (Psalm 28:7, 46:1; 2 Corinthians 12:10). Joni Eareckson Tada knowingly explains, "He does not *willingly*—that is, He doesn't from the heart—bring affliction or grief. Suffering may be a part of God's larger and most mysterious plan, but God's intention is always to demonstrate compassion and unfailing love that touches people at their deepest point of need."[47]

Joni learned to trust God entirely with His plan for her life and believes Romans 8:29 in that He

---

47. Tada, *A Place of Healing*, 61.

foreknew how He would mold her into the likeness of Jesus. She says,

> "Besides all the other reasons for my life, His highest purpose is that I might become gradually conformed to the image of His Son, who lives within me. What of suffering then? What of illness? What of disability? Am I to tell Him which tools He can use and which tools He can't use in the lifelong task of perfecting me and molding me into the beautiful image of Jesus?"[48]

Jesus understands our weaknesses in dealing with the pain and disappointments of life. He says, "Come to Me, all who are weary and heavy-laden, and I will give you rest" (Matthew 11:28–30). I came to understand that I was being refined by the experiences of life both good and bad, both rewarding and disappointing, both physically conquering and physically defeating. The trials I faced with faith, calling on the strength of the Lord, would be rewarded (James 1:12). Through the Scripture, I could see how I was expected in all circumstances to not give up, to strive on in the strength and comfort of the Lord, learning, and teaching others how to do the same.

---

48. Tada, 65–66.

Trusting God with Your Life

Seeing God's Wisdom

Foundational to accepting God's plan for our lives, coinciding with believing God exists, is understanding and accepting that He is an all-wise God. Isaiah said, "His understanding is inscrutable" (40:28b). Webster defines *inscrutable* as "not readily investigated or interpreted: hard to grasp."[49] Often in Scripture, one sees that God reminded His people of His faithfulness and wisdom in dealing with their circumstances. He delivered them from numerous, dangerous situations which required that they walk by faith (Hebrews 11). Many of these situations required trials and suffering. Many prayers were answered in victory, but for some there was suffering even unto death that also served an eternal purpose. The walk of faith in all of these situations required a trust in God's wisdom that was far beyond their own personal understanding. They understood what God declared to Isaiah, "'For My thoughts are not your thoughts, neither are your ways My ways,' declares the Lord" (55:8). Paul explained that the mercy God was providing to all included the Gentiles who were being grafted into an eternal salvation. Paul exclaimed, "Oh, the depth of the riches both of the wisdom and knowledge of God!" (Romans 11:33a). The King James Version of that verse ends with "and His ways past finding out!" (Romans 11:33b). His wis-

---

49. *Websters New Collegiate Dictionary*, 1973 ed., s.v. "inscrutable" (Springfield, MA: G. & C. Merriam Co., 1973).

dom can be trusted with our lives because He has been trustworthy in the past in so many examples in history and in our own personal lives.

The challenges of those saints in the Bible and the numerous examples of men and women throughout history reminded me of my own personal challenges and close encounters with death which God had already brought me through. The pneumonia as a baby, the ruptured appendix at six, the near miss in the path of a log truck, two motorcycle accidents, a car accident, and many other close calls came to mind. Add the poor personal choices in youth which could have plunged me into a life of destruction if it were not for the intervening grace of God.

We all have had our own situations and circumstances which when recalled make it clear the hand of God brought us through, saved our lives, or sustained our health, and guided us to choices leading to our Savior. In trusting an all-wise God and giving Him the credit due for bringing me through life's challenging experiences, I had to trust His hand had been upon me through infertility, also. I had to have faith His divine plan was being perfectly carried out in my life.

Did I Have Enough Faith in God's Wisdom?

Did I have the faith in God required to trust Him? The Bible is clear concerning what faith is and that we cannot please God without it. We know our faith must be the "conviction of things not seen" (Hebrews 11:1b). Many times, we do not fully know or understand how God is using our life and circumstances to draw us closer to Christ our Savior and how our life fits into His overall plan for humankind.

Glimpses of His work and activity can be seen from time to time if one is looking and listening. For example, His work and activity appear when we read the Scripture and consider its application to our lives. We hear the voice of the Holy Spirit from Scripture teaching our hearts with messages of guidance, love, and encouragement. We can notice how God is working in our relationships as we extend the love of Christ to family and friends through acts of kindness and words of love and guidance. We can see how God is holding back the impact of sin and darkness in the world. We can also see how we can be tools in His hands to stand for righteousness and share the love of Jesus before all those who need the light of the gospel.

Our faith will grow as we notice more and more His hand in our lives and the lives of those around us, advancing His Kingdom in the world. I had to remember that my life meant more than whether I could give birth to a child or not. I had to put my trust in God to use me in many other ways. "Trust in the Lord, and do good; dwell in the land and cultivate faithfulness . . . And He will bring forth your righteousness as the light, and your judgment as the noonday" (Psalm 37:3–6).

First of all, I had to believe that God's wisdom is beyond anything I could imagine. In other words, as noted earlier, His wisdom goes farther than any breadth or length that our finite minds can conceive. According to A.W. Tozer, "The idea of God as infinitely wise is at the root of all truth."[50] Now, that is profound when one considers that He is all truth and everything that is absolute in this life is from Him. Everything functions on the foundation of His truth whether we recognize it or not. Tozer compares this wisdom when he says, "But the wisdom of any creature or of all creatures, when set against the boundless wisdom of God, is pathetically small."[51] The adverb *pathetically* refers to how small the quantity, or the quality, for that matter, of our wisdom is, and is quite humbling. Whatever wisdom we possess is but a tiny fraction of the wisdom of God. And, unfortunately, our finite minds even have a way of turning what we think is wisdom into foolishness (1 Corinthians 3:19–20).

So what is *wisdom*? Even in our finite minds, we cannot fully explain it. Tozer explains it probably better than anyone can when he says:

---

50. A.W. Tozer, *The Knowledge of the Holy: The Attributes of God—Their Meaning in the Christian Life* (New York, NY: Harper & Row, 1961), 60.
51. Tozer, *The Knowledge*, 60.

Wisdom, among other things, is the ability to devise perfect ends and to achieve those ends by the most perfect means. It sees the end from the beginning, so there can be no need to guess or conjecture. Wisdom sees everything in focus, each in proper relation to all, and is thus able to work toward predestined goals with flawless precision.[52]

Our focus is blurred. We see "as through a glass darkly" (1 Corinthians 13:12, King James Version) unable to focus and see the big picture concerning the world and how we fit into the purpose of God. Thankfully, through His Word, we see that our most perfect purpose is to trust and worship Him and to "love the Lord your God with all your heart, and with all your soul, and with all your mind" and "love your neighbor as yourself" (Matthew 22:37–39). All that we do should be contained within that concept. How we go about it is guided by Him and we get glimpses of His guiding hand moving us within this purpose in the pages of Scripture.

Accepting God's Will?

Was I willing to accept that it was the will of God for me to be infertile? That is the question that I had to battle with. We all want answers and can be

---
52. Tozer, *The Knowledge*, 60.

rather demanding in expecting them. J.B. Phillips saw mankind as putting demands on God when he explained, "Modern man has a lust for full explanation and habitually considers himself in no way morally bound unless he is in full possession of all the facts. Hence, of course, the prevalence of non-committal agnosticism."[53] In this case, Phillips was referring to man's desire for an answer to the pain, suffering, and evil as part of the fallen world and defining God and His characteristics according to mankind's understanding and expectations.

There are many types of pain and suffering. You might wonder why God allowed infertility in your particular case. Well, I do not blame you for wondering. I wondered but I had to recognize and accept that I will never know until I am with my Father God in heaven. He may reveal, he might not, or it might not matter how my particular disability fits into the scheme of my life and the plan of humankind, altogether. Again, I had to ask if I was willing to accept God's will for my earthly life whether I understood or not.

The portrayal of God being the potter and we the clay in His hands is a familiar one. It seems easy enough to accept at face value until it gets real personal and has a monumental impact in some way in our lives (Isaiah 64:8). It is important that we believe

---

[53]. J.B. Phillips, *Your God Is Too Small* (New York: The Macmillan Company, 1961), 96.

Trusting God with Your Life

that God's plan for us is perfect and is no accident. All imperfection will perish with the final culmination of God's plan when there will be a new heaven and new earth as Tozer makes clear when he says, "Toward all this God is moving with infinite wisdom and perfect precision of action. No one can dissuade Him from His purposes; nothing can turn Him aside from His plans. Since He is omniscient, there can be no unforeseen circumstances; no accidents."[54]

Asking why things have to happen to us, since we may consider ourselves some minor players in his plan, does not resolve the question. We are not minor players. Each member of the body of Christ is crucial and has an important role and is not to be seen as minor in any way. In fact, Paul told the Corinthians that those members which "seem to be weaker are necessary" (1 Corinthians 12:22b) and goes on to say, "But God has so composed the body, giving more abundant honor to that member which lacked" (1 Corinthians 12:24b).

Our real problem is that we do not want to accept that God chose this condition for us. We are rebellious in being obedient to accept His will. Our emotions take over and all we can see is something we want that has been denied. According to Bridges, our emotions take over our reason. He explains, "The will has become stubborn and rebellious and will not consent to that which reason knows to be the will of

---

54. Tozer, *The Knowledge of the Holy*, 111–112.

God. Or, more commonly, the emotions get the upper hand and draw away both reason and will from obedience to God."[55]

Was it possible that God chose me and other women specifically for this particular type of disability? I had to consider that He may be using the disability of infertility because it has certain ramifications that could draw me closer in my relationship with Him as well as also impact those around me in a life-changing way. The answers, again, were far beyond my understanding, but I had to trust Him that they were valuable and beneficial. R.T. Kendall wrote, "It may not seem that way now. But I can tell you that if there is anything that has been clear to me, it is this. We will be eternally grateful in heaven for our particular thorn. For there is a definite, thought-out reason why God has done this. It is to drive us closer to Him, not further from Him."[56] I had to consider that I may have been chosen, special, and privileged to receive a role in life which has eternal purposes. This perspective required that I had to work at being thankful and grateful in order to receive peace and purpose in my life.

---

55. Bridges, *The Pursuit*, 100.
56. R.T. Kendall, *The Thorn in the Flesh* (Lake Mary, FL: Charisma House, 2004), 102.

Blessings Instead of Disappointments

I had to begin to look for blessings despite what I saw as disappointments. As I looked with eyes of gratitude, I found there were far more blessings than disappointments. Paul reminded Timothy that "everything created by God is good" and should be "received with gratitude" (1 Timothy 4:4). Appreciating even the smallest miracles of life from the tiniest creature and flower to the awesome expanse of the sky and a golden sunset became a new goal. As the old saying goes, it was important to, "Stop and smell the roses." What I saw as a weakness or loss might have been the incentive to appreciate life more fully in a different but still special way to the glory of God. Appreciating and glorifying God despite life's challenges opens our hearts more fully to His amazing gift of our Savior. God loves us so much that He wants us to fully understand that His gift to us in and through Christ is far beyond just a head knowledge. Getting my focus off what I did not have and on what tremendous blessings I did have changed my entire perspective on the purpose of life.

Do Not Allow Anger and Bitterness to Control You

Jesus wanted me to experience real joy, not some partial joy mixed with lingering anger and bitterness, which could not happen unless I abide in His love with gratitude. Only by abiding in His love would my life produce fruit to the glory of God. How does one abide in His love? Jesus said, "If you abide in Me, and My words abide in you, ask whatever you wish, and it shall be done for you" (John 15:7). He also said, "By this is My Father glorified, that you bear much fruit, and so prove to be My disciples" (John 15:8). Abiding in Him, consuming His words, and keeping His commandments are prerequisites for bearing fruit and experiencing joy (John 15:9–10). The more I abide in Him and His word, the more my life will bear fruit. My joy was being made full and complete as I became more capable of enduring the trial of infertility or any disappointment. James reminded me in his epistle that enduring trials is nothing but "all joy" since through the testing of my faith I could be "perfect and complete, lacking in nothing" (James 1:2–4). That is an incredible promise! If I was lacking in nothing, then, how could any disappointment stand in my way or cause me to feel any regret or sorrow?

John Piper tells us that joy is part of our duty. This duty is not a half-hearted attempt but is expected fully in all circumstances as Paul declares, "Rejoice always" (1 Thessalonians 5:16) and James directs, "Consider it all joy" (James 1:2). Notice the words *always* and *all*. This is entirely clear in that there are no times or circumstances in which we should be joyless. Piper explains that in all situations we cannot "water down" these commands or expect a half duty response.[57]

Accepting Suffering as Christ Did

Thirty-three years old; young in our world. Yet, He laid His agenda aside, died to self on a daily basis, and then sacrificed Himself for others. We complain when someone cuts in front of us in line at the grocery, when we might have to miss a meal, or we do not get enough sleep. This is why it is so difficult to accept a plan for our life that does not seem to fit our idea. We want to have what we think everyone else has; a nice house, latest car, loving spouse, two or three loving children, good looks throughout our life with few signs of aging, and plenty of financial resources to buy and do whatever fits our fancy.

Even though the Bible expounds on the joys and rewards of children, I had to ask, "Does it really claim that this blessing is for everyone and that everyone will receive it?", "Does the Bible claim that a person is cursed if they do not have this blessing?", and "Does the Bible promise us anything more than the joy of salvation and eternal happiness with God?" I think I knew the answer. In plain terms, this world is not our home and we should not expect everything to be roses or everything to be about us. Of course,

---

57. John Piper, *When the Darkness Will Not Lift: Doing What We Can While We Wait for God and Joy* (Wheaton, IL: Crossway Books, 2006), 49.

there are the joys of God's wonderful creation, the joy of relationships, and the peace of walking with confidence in the Lord. Should I really expect more? Human nature is to want more no matter how much we possess. It was a stark reminder to me to consider that our Lord and Savior did not even have a place of His own to lay His head.

Considering What God Was Saying

Was God sending me a message? After months and years of failed pregnancy attempts, I had to come to the realization that God must be sending a message. For whatever reason, the message must be that pregnancy and childbirth were not in my future but that He had another plan for my life and life with my spouse. This message was difficult to accept. However, God who gave me a beautiful world to live in, provided for my basic needs and more, sent me a Savior, gave me the Holy Spirit for guidance and comfort, and promised to provide me an eternal home, is also the same God who could be trusted with a beautiful plan for my life. He was telling me to accept His plan and not consider it to be less valuable or rewarding. Otherwise, I would be judging my God as incapable of knowing what is best, incapable of providing a better plan for me, incapable of being a loving and caring God. I believe the God of Scripture looked at me and looks at each one of us as unique and special and has a perfect plan for our good and not for our demise (Jeremiah 29:11).

All too often, I have compared my life to others and thought I had missed out on something. But, I had to learn to appreciate that God's plan for me as an individual was unique and special. Only then could I appreciate that God's plan for others is unique and special to them, also. More and more, I appreciated the uniqueness of the life God had given me and did not covet the life of others. God knows me better than I do myself. He knows why He created me the way I am and what His plan is for me. He knew what I was able to bear. No other life could be a substitute for what I could bear in what He had planned for me. He knew who my life would impact and how my experiences would impact me for my good and for His glory. Be thankful because He gives us what He knows we can bear (1 Corinthians 10:13) and reminds us, "Cast your burden upon the Lord, and He will sustain you; He will never allow the righteous to be shaken" (Psalm 55:22). We need to look for the diamonds and treasures of joy and uniqueness He has just for us. Appreciate and celebrate what others have been given but do not covet those things. By walking in their shoes, we might discover that the situations and conditions that they are bearing would be totally destructive to us and not at all the life God had planned for our growth in Christ Jesus.

There came a time for me as an infertile woman to relax in the beautiful plan God has for me. There came a time when I had to look to the future with joy and expectation of the gifts and purpose He had for me. The door opened to new and exciting opportunities. For us, personally, one opportunity was the possibility of adoption that became a consideration. For others, this may or may not be a consideration. Perhaps another woman or couple is called to a rewarding ministry which requires the dedication of time and commitment. Perhaps a rewarding career of service is awaiting others. Each couple must listen to the voice of God and then decide what adventure ahead awaits them. Together, God will show them a way to complement each other and contribute to their lives as one and to the world around them.

As we began seeking God's new and special purpose for us, He opened the door for us to adopt. After a great deal of thought and research, covered in prayer, we were provided with an opportunity to bring a little toddler into our home. Chapter eight not only describes our experience but will give insight into the joys and difficulties of adoption. Since adoption is often, at least, a consideration for an infertile couple, you will want to see how we, by the grace of God, navigated through this experience in our life in the pages ahead.

CHAPTER EIGHT

IS ADOPTION IN THE PLAN?

As an infertile couple considers the future, there often comes a time when adoption of a child becomes an option to think about and consider seriously. Adoption can certainly be an exciting prospect, restoring hope in fulfilling the desire to parent a child. However, there are several considerations to take into account. It's important for a couple to consider their motivation and all the ramifications and circumstances of introducing an infant or child into a home that has been childless for usually an extended period of time. For instance, we had to consider whether we were mentally and spiritually ready for a child that we did not bear but for whom we most likely had some preconceived expectations. Along with the potential joys, were we aware of the potential difficulties surrounding most adoptees statistically known to experience some past level of trauma? These may seem rather ominous, possibly challenging considerations, but child-rearing in itself is a great undertaking requiring a full-time commitment and a great deal of mental and spiritual strength.

Adoption adds to child-rearing an additional level of potential emotional and relational ramifications that one might not have considered. We certainly weren't as prepared as we should have been. Consequently, it is highly recommended to become fully educated, not only in the process but also in the experience of adoption. There are several more resources available now than there were ten or twenty years ago. Christian couples will want to carefully analyze the literature and access a more Bible-based perspective on adoption issues and approaches rather than a strictly, secular, psychology-based perspective. There is some common sense advice in secular literature. Still, one would want to look at the research carefully, especially in the areas of behavior identification, labeling, and therapies for adopted children. Overall, as one ponders adoption, approach the possibility with much prayer, contemplation, and discussion as priorities.

Before moving forward with adoption, we had to settle in our minds, unreservedly, whether God's choice for us was to raise a child or remain childless. Any infertile couple must come to a full resolution in their minds and hearts whether pursuing a child they have not conceived or whether remaining childless is the right path for them. God is sovereign and has designed a plan for each one that fulfills His purpose.

Is Adoption in the Plan?

Jerry Bridges reminds us that there are no surprises with God. "We make plans but are often forced to change those plans. But there are no contingencies with God. Our unexpected, forced change of plans is a part of His plan."[58] Consequently, consideration should have already been given to the possibility that God may actually plan for a couple to be childless and, thus, be available for some task for which they are perfectly suited and would be of great benefit in God's providential work.

Many people have been used, sacrificially, in Christian ministry, missionary assignments, or even in science, education, service roles, or other worthy endeavors which have providentially advanced the physical and/or spiritual welfare of mankind. In this case, the longing for a child and typical family life may still hold a strong draw, but overriding that draw can be a great satisfaction experienced in a life calling that compensates for childlessness. Once a childless couple in a full-time life calling has resolved that being childless is not a punishment but in God's providential plan for them, life can be pursued with new joy.

---

58. Jerry Bridges, *Trusting God, Even When Life Hurts* (Colorado Springs, CO: NavPress, Tyndale House, 2008), 37.

Important Considerations

If a couple decides to go ahead with adoption, there are several points to consider and questions to answer before proceeding. For instance, adoptions can be facilitated through a state agency, arranged privately with an attorney or through a private agency, and may be arranged either in one's own country or overseas. Adoptions can require minimal cost, as would be the case through a state agency, or cost in the thousands of dollars for private, domestic, or international adoptions.

Considerations must be given as to the relationship parameters between the adoptive and biological family, determining whether the adoption should be "open," "semi-open," or "closed." This is important in reference to how much contact is desired or expected with the biological family while the child is being raised and, in the future, including whether medical information and genealogical heritage are provided. The current trend is for open adoptions, which literature seems to show results in a more well-adjusted adoptee. The impact of and on an adopted child of the immediate, adopted family, especially if there are already children in the family, and the environment of the extended family, should also be considered.

The presence of emotional trauma in the background of the adoptee, normally present to some degree, as well as possible physical abuse, neglect, drug and alcohol exposure, and disabilities are all likely, in one way or another, to impact the emotional and/or physical well-being of the child. Some of these concerns may require additional patience and special training. The emotional strength of the adoptive mother and father as well as the overall strength of the marriage make a huge difference in the success of the adoption since adoption will require a special understanding and response to possible traumatic factors in the child's background.

There will be definite physical and emotional adjustments to be considered for both the adoptee, adoptive parents, and other children in the home. If the adjustment is too difficult, it can result in further pain for the adoptee and the adoptive parents. The adoptee has already experienced the loss of their biological parents and family, regardless of the circumstances. Adoptive parents have suffered the loss of their fertility and often experienced years of childlessness. These losses for the adoptee and adoptive parents can result in potential emotional instability.

Couples should consider whether they want to focus on a baby or whether they would consider a toddler or an older child, since infants are not as readily available. Will the couple consider sibling groups or only single children? These and the other issues presented do not consist of the entire scope of possible concerns but are a place to begin discussion. Some further detail will be presented on each of these issues.

The Adoption Process

To begin the adoption process requires some research. The library and the Internet are good places to access most of the information needed regarding state or private adoption agencies and associations. Other adoptive parents are excellent resources on sources for adoption and also all the particular experiences one might face in the process. Once a list of sources has been established, it is then a matter of studying the application processes and requirements, the policies and procedures, the cost of adoption from each source, and then making a comparative list. After narrowing down the list, it would be helpful to make an appointment with the agencies and get a better, firsthand idea of what is involved along with the difficulties one might face with the timeline and types of issues possible with the adoptees.

Private adoptions, as mentioned, especially through private agencies, can be quite expensive and prohibitive, requiring a large investment. Some couples take out a second mortgage or run up their credit card to cover the costs. Consequently, it is always a good idea to make your request for a child known to your pastor and other community pastors, your doctor and others, especially obstetricians, pregnancy resource centers, and maternity homes. Our daughter came to us through our pastor's brother-in-law's relatives. It was a simple, no-contest adoption,

Is Adoption in the Plan?

handled through a private attorney with adoption experience and a heart for keeping the cost down. This is not always the case. A home study was still required through the state children's services agency. Overall, the process took only a few months to complete. These types of adoptions are somewhat uncommon but the more widely you circulate your adoption desire, the more possibility an available child will be made known in this or a similar manner.

Babies are difficult to find due to the high number of abortions performed every year. Some couples seeking to adopt go through months and years of searching through state and private adoption resources for a child that fits their desire, family situation, and lifestyle. Especially, if their goal is to find an infant, the availability is low and there is a great deal of competition.

Our daughter was two years old before her young biological mother decided to relinquish rights. By that time, the mother had only been in her life off and on, leaving her often with a grandmother, great-grandmother, and finally with a great-uncle and great-aunt. Her biological mother had struggled to make room for her daughter in her teen life and had trouble making decisions about her daughter's future. Even though she endured a very unstable first two years of her life, we are thankful that her mother gave her life and finally made the decision to allow her to live in our home.

In a private adoption, the rights of the mother and the father have to be relinquished. If the father is not available, an attempt to contact him is still required. Our attorney posted a notice about our intention to adopt in a couple of newspapers which is all that was required in Oregon. If the biological father does not contact the attorney and contest the adoption, then the adoption proceeds based on the biological mother's relinquishment of rights. The attorney takes care of all of the legal procedures required for relinquishment of rights of both parents.

All adoptions require a home study which involves a visit to the home from a state adoption worker and interviews with family members and, sometimes, extended family members. This should not be a threatening requirement. One can obtain some specifics on what an agency is expecting and it may also be helpful to talk with other adoptive parents regarding their home study experience. Expect, at least, in this meeting to provide information regarding marriage stability, personal history, financial status, employment status, relationships with relatives, and parenting philosophy. Most states do not accept a philosophy of corporal punishment of any kind and expect adoptive parents to have an idea of how they would handle behavior issues. Adoption agencies are not looking for a "perfect" home, if there is such a thing, but a loving and secure atmosphere.

Is Adoption in the Plan?

The questions and paperwork of a home study may seem overwhelming. Some couples have difficulty with all the personal information they are required to submit. Often, the application process and home study take months to complete. For some, the whole process may seem like a never-ending ordeal. Julie Irwin Zimmerman experienced firsthand what she knows most couples think about the process. She says, "It might seem like it's just not worth the hassle, especially if they've endured years of trying to conceive."[59] The entire process requires a lot of patience in most cases. Since we already had an adoptee referred to us, an attorney getting all the legal requirements put in place, and we lived in the county seat of a relatively small, rural community, the home study was expedited and completed in a rather short amount of time.

Some states require a couple to foster children first and some highly encourage it before being accepted as an adoptive couple. Foster parents go through special training for understanding the trauma that most children experience prior to entering foster care. Private and overseas adoptions do not have this requirement. Either way, becoming certified as a foster care provider and taking in some children may be an excellent way for a couple to determine what it would be like to introduce a child into their home. It may be helpful to ask the state adoption agency to

---

59. Zimmerman, *A Spiritual Companion*, 154.

connect a couple with some foster parents they could visit in person to get a better understanding of what a foster care experience would be like.

Once a couple has completed the entire application process and has been approved to adopt a child, the wait can normally be months or years. Overseas adoptions can require visits to the agency and orphanage in the foreign country. Some couples have to wait in the foreign country before final approval to take the child with them. After a child is placed in the home, there are still many visits from the adoption agency social worker to make sure all is going well. Finally, after the adoption waiting period is completed, the adoption can be legally finalized.

Even after the finalization of an adoption, the birth mother or father, in some cases, might change their mind and try to retrieve the child. There have been cases where a biological parent was successful but the percentages of that happening are low. However, biological parents can present a convincing case sometimes and threaten to disrupt and overturn the adoption. Fortunately, these cases are rare but they can cause fear and concern. Most of all, these concerns and all the circumstances in an adoption must be approached with trust in a sovereign God who will bring about the perfect situation and outcome. We are reminded by Jerry Bridges, "As we seek God's glory, we may be sure that He has purposed our good and that He will not be frustrated in fulfilling that purpose."[60]

What Should We Expect?

There is nothing more wonderful than to be heading home with your adopted child and hear the child say, "Hi, Mommy," as was the case with our two-year-old adopted daughter. She was so ready to have her own "Mommy and Daddy" and be away from the foster home where she was told not to call the "aunt" foster mother "Mommy." The experience of her expressing happiness in being with her new parents and our joy in having her with us was totally beyond anything we had experienced in our lives. After six years of childless marriage, we embarked on a wonderful adventure with expectations of immeasurable happiness.

Without reservation, the younger years, for the most part, were a happy and joyful time raising our daughter. There were a few concerns along the way but nothing we thought was unusual for any parenting experience. Looking back, we can identify some signs of the emotional stress and scars that we learned can be expected with any child experiencing the trauma of the loss of their biological family. But being new parents and having little information on what to expect, we went about raising our daughter

---

60. Bridges, *Trusting God*, 43.

with the joy, naïve bliss, and love characteristic of most new parents.

However, we did notice some lack of closeness and bonding concerns between us and experienced some worry over how our daughter related with others. We thought these concerns could be overcome in time. We thought life would continue fairly uneventfully. We did not take as seriously as we should have the expressions and body language we saw in the first pictures of her right after we brought her home. There was a fear and apprehension in her eyes and, early on, a standoffish attitude that we did not fully understand at the time. Hugging was resisted or only allowed for short periods. There was a territorial attitude toward playthings and playmates in groups of other children. Some of her reactions were to be expected. We were not totally surprised when we tried to imagine ourselves in her situation. However, we thought she would get over the impact fairly quickly. Little did we know that these and other signs were a natural and deep-seated response to the reality shock of another drastic change in her life, a resistance to trust that was already well-honed, a protective resistance to bonding, and a fear of being hurt once again. Her hurtful past experiences and reactions did not go away easily or completely and would later cause tension and distance between us.

After the first few days, our adopted daughter seemed to be comfortable enough with us as the

Is Adoption in the Plan?

huge change began to sink in and became accepted, at least it appeared so. She must have been overwhelmed with her own room, new clothes, more toys than she had ever known, and an onslaught of attention from an incredible number of strangers. But it all had to have been so surreal in ways her little, two-year-old mind could not begin to comprehend. One could see now how it would take her years to sort it all out.

It is to be expected that when couples decide to adopt, they are thrilled with a baby or child to bring into their home and rear as their own. It is easy to become attached to a little one that needs consistent love and care. This can be a fulfilling experience with many lifelong rewards for the couple and the child. However, as stated, many adoptions come with difficulties due to the pain, hurt, abuse, abandonment, and sometimes physical impairments from drugs and alcohol which the child carries with them to their new family. Even if the preadoption experience of the adoptee was not severe, as in the case of physical/emotional abuse or alcohol or drug syndromes, the abandonment and disruptive early years can cause adjustment issues and some mental health concerns.

Mental Health of Adoptees

Studies of adoptions since the 1950s have shown a large number of adoptees needing mental health care. "A study at the University of Minnesota found that adopted children have almost doubled odds of having contact with a mental health professional and having a disruptive behavior disorder."[61] Even for a baby, abandonment becomes more and more of an issue as the child struggles, especially as a teen, with their concern and questions about their genealogical and biological family. GinaMarie Guarino of the Claudia Black Young Adult Center points out in saying,

> Twelve to fourteen percent of adopted children in the United States between the ages of eight and eighteen are diagnosed with a mental health disorder each year, and adopted children are almost twice as likely as children brought up with their biological parents to suffer from mood disorders like anxiety, depression, and behavioral issues.[62]

---

61. Kristen Fuller, "Adopted Children More Likely to Develop Mental Health Disorders, Study Shows," Soveregin Health, November 9, 2016, accessed February 19, 2019, https://www.sovhealth.com/mental-health/adopted-children-likely-developmental-health-disorders-study-shows/.
62. GinaMarie Guarino, "Adopted Children Often Face Mental Health Struggles as Young Adults," Claudia Black Young Adult Center, May 30, 2017, accessed February 19, 2019, https://www.claudiablackcenter.com/adopted-children-often-face-mental-health-struggles-as-young-adults/

Is Adoption in the Plan?

Some of the factors, Guarino identifies as contributing to mental health disorders, are the "age of adoption, where the child was adopted from, conditions of the foster home and family, whether the child has contact with his or her biological family members (Open Adoption), and history of mental illness in biological family."[63] These studies have found that these and other contributing factors are directly related to the serious adjustment problems that can even cause the adoptee to turn against their adoptive parents.

Many adoptees do not bond in the same way with the adoptive parents as they would with the biological parents. When we noticed our adopted daughter would not allow us to hug her or pushed away quickly and did not respond in kind to a hug, we recognized there was a definite wall. If this wall is present, it can become more prominent as the child enters adolescence and does not decrease but becomes more pronounced in the teen years. With each disagreement or need for correction, the child may further resist bonding in an effort to maintain a wall of protection around a perceived threat or hurt. Some of the issues that develop due to inadequate bonding and attachment, according to GinaMarie Gaurino, are "self-esteem issues, anxiety, depression, self-harm,

---

63. Guarino, "Adopted Children Often Face Mental Health Struggles."

behavioral issues, academic struggles, and difficulty building meaningful relationships."[64]

It may be difficult to understand why a little child, still so young and innocent, could be so severely impacted by the conditions they may have experienced. But abandonment along with all the potential issues of "divorce, physical abuse, drug and alcohol abuse, instability, and other crises in the child's natural family drastically impair the child's welfare and adjustment to the adoptive family," as Julie Smith Lowe points out. The fallen condition of our world explains why, she says, "These children's stories always begin with broken relationships. They have difficulty in accurately making sense of their own life situation." Lowe emphasizes that these children have no grounding to make sense of their world. Most of them have no understanding about what, she says, "God says about Himself, our world, and ourselves. Without that reference point, we draw faulty conclusions about ourselves, God, and our life experiences. We become the center of our own world and act accordingly."[65] To adoptees, at an early age, life seems unfair, confusing, and full of potential hurts and rejections. The adoptee's response is often from a fear of losing what little security they perceive they have and not trusting the adults in their lives who they

---

64. Guarino, "Adopted Children."
65. Julie Smith Lowe, "Counseling the Adopted Child," *The Journal of Biblical Counseling* 25, 3 (Winter 2007): 38, https://www.ccef.org/shop/product/jbc-volume-25-1-pdf/.

Is Adoption in the Plan?

perceive could potentially hurt them or place them in another vulnerable situation. Acting out in extreme ways or, in other cases, withdrawing, can seem to be one's means of self-protection.

Regardless of what one reads or hears about adoptees, it's important to remember that, just like all children, they are individuals with different backgrounds, experiences, and personalities. Diagnoses can be overused and are only a means for those in the helping professions to communicate regarding an adoptees' behavior or maladjustment. Dawn Davenport warns that diagnoses become popular such as in the case of reactive attachment disorder, which is a diagnosis describing the way a child responds in a form of withdrawal and inability to bond due to trauma. However, a child may become overdiagnosed or be diagnosed before there is enough history to really understand the child who may change depending on the setting in which the child is living. Davenport clarifies this diagnosis dilemma in saying,

> That is not to say that some adopted children do not have serious or persistent mental health problems. Rather, we want parents to be careful about accepting historical or even current diagnoses if their experience with the child does not match the diagnosis. Treat

children as individuals, not as their diagnoses.[66]

There was the assumption, thirty or forty years ago, that if an orphan child was rescued from an abandoned, neglected, or abusive situation that all would be bliss for them when they entered an adoptive home. Other than a slight adjustment, it was thought they would appreciate their home and adoptive parents as they grew up and would have little thought about their biological family or desire to connect with them. Studies have shown, however, that this is not the case. Studies indicate that most adoptees go through an identity crisis and do not feel complete or whole until they are able to reconnect with their biological family and resolve, in their mind, the circumstances of their adoption. As adoptees mature and try to make sense of who they are and their circumstances, they begin to ask questions about their origin, family heritage, and why their mother and her family gave them up.

Impact of the Biological Family

Our daughter wanted to meet her biological mother before she left home at eighteen years old. With some reluctance and discussion with her, we

---

66. Dawn Davenport, "Mental Health of Adoptees," Creating a Family, May 23, 2016, accessed February 19, 2019, https://creatingafamily.org/adoption-category/mental-health-adoptees/.

Is Adoption in the Plan?

decided to go ahead and arranged the visit through family members we still knew how to reach. The biological mother and grandmother attended the visit. The experience answered some of our daughter's questions about family resemblances, her siblings she had never met, the circumstances in the family before the adoption, and included a few pictures and stories about her as a baby and toddler. It was positive in the sense that it answered some questions we couldn't answer for her, but it didn't fully answer "why" she was given up. As parents, we were open to understanding their situation during our daughter's infant years and thankful our daughter was made available to us but also shocked over the excuses given by the biological family for giving her up. Later, we tried to gently explain the difficulties her biological family had expressed in the visit to our daughter but understandably felt like it was still not justified in her mind, consequently not easing her feelings of rejection. Although she could see all the difficulties and negative circumstances that could have impacted her life so differently, environmentally, she also expressed disappointment in being biologically connected to a family with many serious concerns she thought might also genetically affect her. Even though it upset her to know the negative details about her biological family, it still didn't seem to make her more thankful to be adopted.

Actually, adoptees may resent adoptive parents and blame them partially for coming between them and the possibility, in their minds, of some reconciliation with their biological parents and/or family. This resentment has been known to be directed primarily toward the adoptive mother who they see would dare to try to replace their real mother. According to Mary Ostyn, "The hard truth is that *every* child who doesn't get to grow up with his first mom has experienced traumatic loss . . . every wound along the way will impact his ability to accept love and enjoy a healthy, reciprocal relationship."[67]

In our personal case, neglect and abandonment were the issues that impacted our daughter, the effects of which were especially evident as she reached adolescence. As we studied the literature made available in later years, we discovered that some of the relationship issues we had in the teen years could be traced to a lack of bonding between us. As mentioned earlier, child psychology calls this "reactive attachment disorder." Whatever label one wants to put on it really does not matter, it is just a number of reactions to a lack of bonding. The bottom line is that the child has not bonded and attached to the parents in as deep a way as would have occurred in a healthy, biological relationship. When conflict arises or correction needs to be given, the child recoils in an attempt to protect themselves from what they see

---

67. Ostyn, *Forever Mom*, 17.

Is Adoption in the Plan?

as rejection and control. A child who has not bonded and does not trust others will want to retain personal control. While some children may react by attempting to overplease to retain control and not be rejected, others will pull into themselves, become resentful, and turn against the adoptive parents. During the home study interviews, we were given an offhanded warning about adopted children creating protective barriers and striving to maintain control as two areas of potential concern. The adoption worker told us that adopted children will often throw up an emotional barrier if they feel they are backed into a corner. Adopted children may protect their feelings in tending to show little emotion, tenderness, and expression of feelings. When corrected, they may react defensively and become bitter, rarely admitting any wrong or sorrow over the matter.

> All adopted children, even those adopted at birth, know subconsciously that they have been separated from the source of their biological being. They have experienced a trauma as real as any tragedy in life. It goes to the very depth of their being and cannot be easily overcome. The bond with the biological mother they forged in the womb has been torn from them and no one can replace what they sense or

know to be that true motherly bond. Nancy Verrier, adoption therapist, calls it the "primal wound."[68]

The biological mother may have even been neglectful or abusive but yet the child still feels an attachment and bond that cannot be fully replaced. There will always be questions also about the biological father, his role in the mother's life, and in abandoning both the mother and the child. However, the real issue is that the adoptive mother will never be a replacement for the bond the child felt with their biological mother. The longer they were together after birth, before the adoption, the deeper the detachment pain will be, especially if the young child was not abused. They cannot rationalize in their minds why their mother has disappeared from their lives and will blame themselves for her leaving them. In writing from the view of an adoptee who studied adoption, Betty Jean Lifton captures the questioning focus of an adoptee's thoughts, in saying:

> The adopted child is always accompanied by the ghost of the child he might have been had he stayed with his birth mother and by the ghost of the fantasy child his adoptive parents might have had. He is also accompanied by the

---

68. Nancy N. Verrier, *The Primal Wound: Understanding the Adopted Child* (San Diego, CA: Nancy Verrier Publications, 1993).

Is Adoption in the Plan?

ghost of the birth mother, from whom he has never completely disconnected, and the ghost of the birth father, hidden behind her.[69]

Consequences of Lack of Bonding

The reluctance or inability to attach could be classified as serious as any post-traumatic stress disorder in the sense that it disrupts the stability of the child. This is evidenced as they mature and the way they react to life's setbacks, failures, relationship issues and conflicts, personal view of self, and circumstances of which one has little control. If not addressed at a young age, lack of attachment can result in adjustment issues in forming lasting bonds. For instance, lack of attachment can contribute to a higher degree of relationship issues, divorce, possible drug and alcohol abuse, inability to establish successful life goals, inability to see value in their talents or skills, and the likelihood of passing on emotional detachment to their children.

It is true that everyone has difficulties and failures and may not feel accepted by others at different points in life. However, as is true of everyone, it is how one reacts and if one is able to see oneself as a valuable creation of God with a purpose and

---

69. Betty Jean Lifton, *Journey of the Adopted Self: A Quest for Wholeness* (New York, NY: Basic Books, 1994), 11.

plan regardless of how one's life began. Many adoptees have difficulty overcoming the concept of being given a raw deal, so to speak. They see themselves as continuing to be victimized by several people in their lives they see as not accepting them. The adoptee believes others see them as tainted and not able to live up to some cultural ideal. Consequently, due to a perceived stigma and victim mentality, a lack of bonding can result in a rebellious and laissez-faire attitude toward pleasing adoptive parents, others in authority, and a lack of respect for the adoptive parents in their parenting decisions and approach. Since they see themselves as victims, they rarely take responsibility for their own contribution to conflicts or negative incidents and for any bad attitudes. These can be detrimental factors when the child tries to exert independence and form their own identity. All children come to a point where they challenge their parent's authority and desire to make many of their own, independent decisions. In either case, however, whether adopted or not, the parent's guidance is usually respected more when there is a solid bond between them and the child. There is more respect for the parents when there is no identity crisis in the child, wondering who they really are or who they may have been, had they not been adopted.

Parenting conflicts with adoptees do not discount the fact that the adoptive parents may lack parenting skills, especially if the adopted child is their first

Is Adoption in the Plan?

child. The adoptive parents may lack skill and understanding in how to bond with the child or how to address some disagreements, especially in the teen years. Abandonment or other emotional trauma prior to adoption will cause adopted children to react differently to punishment and denial of privileges. As stated, they have a tendency to build walls to protect themselves from anything they perceive as rejection. Rejection to them results in possible future abandonment which they perceive they may not emotionally survive.

Trust for adoptees is a fragile commodity, one which can easily be reduced by what they perceive to be an attack on their worthiness in this world. They may believe the biological mother or family was unhappy with them and could not love them unconditionally. It is easy for adoptees to transfer the perception of past displeasure onto the adoptive parents. Any sign of displeasure from the adoptive parents may trigger the possibility in the adoptee's mind that being given up again is a possibility. The lack of understanding and skill on the part of the adoptive parents can cause what is already a fragile trust situation to be even worse. The adoptive parents probably do not even understand all the issues the adoptee is dealing with when the adoptee reacts in a way that does not seem normal or appropriate to the situation.

A lack of bonding, distrust, self-protective, and sometimes self-deprecating attitudes will be exhibited in various ways in the adoptee as they mature. These characteristics might show up initially in hoarding and hiding little treasures, covering up mistakes by hiding evidence, telling lies to cover up a mistake, or in deliberate disobedient behavior. The adoptive parent may also notice a possessive attitude with friends and toys, a territorial, protective response. This attitude is displayed in requiring a friend to be loyal and not play with anyone else. Group play is rarely successful as sharing a perceived friend is often seen as taboo. A toy is not normally shared very readily. The adopted child is likely to stay in the back of a group and observe rather than join in because they perceive themselves as not being worthy or accepted. The child may take something they perceive as special that they do not possess because they already feel like they've been deprived of the best. Jealousy of talents or popularity of others is evident at a young age. There is often a disregard for their own abilities and talents and a jealousy for those of others. Relationships are often broken over the slightest perception of breaking trust. Also, the inability to be a team player and encourage others to be successful is difficult. Parents are tolerated and given little attention and little desire for closeness is shown.

Is Adoption in the Plan?

All of these personal characteristics and attitudes can become more pronounced, if not resolved, as the child enters the teen years. Unfortunately, no matter how hard we tried, some of these attitudes were difficult for us to overcome and we did not see the seriousness of them until teen and adult years. These characteristics may not be true of all adoptees but are not uncommon. Each situation is different depending on the adoptee's emotional and environmental experiences leading up to the adoption. With dedication and spiritual guidance, for many adoptions, trauma consequences can be overcome and a loving, bonded family can be formed. As Lifton reassuringly says,

> "Yet, clinicians are not writing off adopted children when they speak about trauma; rather, they are describing a vulnerability that responsible parents should be aware of. Adopted babies, like all infants, can be tremendously resilient if given the chance, but they have experienced a profound loss that other babies are spared."[70]

One must still keep in mind that if the adoption experience has difficulties and is unfulfilling, it can also throw the infertile, adoptive parents back into

---

70. Lifton, *Journey of the Adopted Self*, 32.

feelings of disappointment. Our inability to produce a child we perceived would have bonded deeply with us and returned love was still an unfortunate circumstance of our lives. Adoption did not fully alleviate the pain of infertility for us. Also, especially for the adoptive mother, the realization that she cannot be a perfect, mother-substitute for the adopted child becomes another painful awareness which leaves her unfulfilled. Looking back, we realized that we hadn't fully comprehended or dealt with our infertility before the adoption. I, especially, hadn't let go of the dream of a biological child and didn't realize how that may have impacted the adoption. Mary Ostyn advises by saying, "If we come to adoption through infertility, we're already intimate with loss , , , But our grief issues can also leave us less emotionally able to walk with our children through their losses"[71]

If the adult adoptee has difficulties adjusting to adulthood, the adoptive parents can become the focus of blame. Regardless of the adoptive parent's positive or negative parenting skills, it can become easy for the adoptee to blame the adoptive parents for perceived gaps in the adoptee's preparation for life. If blaming and accepting responsibility are issues for the adoptee, then, anything the adoptee thinks were mistakes made in how he/she was raised or choices that were made become excuses for not looking at their own maladjustment issues. Along

---

71. Ostyn, *Forever Mom*, 17.

Is Adoption in the Plan?

with inadequate bonding, in many cases, the stage is set for a strained or possibly an estranged relationship which only further damages the adoptee and the adoptive parents. The devastating result is an adoptive couple with the unfulfilled dream of a close relationship with their adopted child and an adoptee who may struggle their entire life with the fantasy of what might have been.

Is Adoption Worth It?

Adoption can be a fulfilling and rewarding alternative to having a biological child. Even if the child is not an infant, a quick attachment of the parents to the child can take place and substitute for a close, biological attachment. Every adoption experience is different. For the most part, adoption is beneficial both for the adoptive parents and the adoptee. With adequate preparation, adoption should always be considered if one is not able to give birth to a child but still longs to raise a child.

However, the childless couple should not go into adoption with blinders on thinking adoption will be the perfect answer to fulfill their dreams of raising a child. Raising children, biological or adopted, is an awesome task. Be willing to accept whatever the experience brings but do not be naïve to think that the experience will be exactly the same as bearing a child, biologically. For instance, you may have to face the realization that your adopted child is different from you in personality and likes and dislikes. An adopted child will pick up some of your mannerisms and way of doing things but you will notice definite differences as a result of their biological and environmental experience contributing to their manner of mental functioning. Surprisingly, people said that our adopted child looked like us as her mannerisms took on a comparable physical resemblance and also since there were similarities in nationality and body structure. When someone, knowingly or not, tells you how much your child looks like you or your husband, you often just say, "Thank you," with a knowing look at each other and a smile. It is nice to hear that your adopted child looks like you but you know that it is just the child acquiring some similar characteristics. However, even though a child takes on some of their parent's personality characteristics, there may be a greater degree of personality differences when one does not share genetics, background, and as the child forms their own identity. Be prepared to possibly hear from one's adopted child as I did, "Mom, I'm not like you," as your child develops their own identity and discerns there are personality characteristics that may come from their biological family.

Adoption can fill the void of infertility and be totally rewarding for many couples. However, even though there is much joy in having a child that is accepted no different than a biological child, there will be reminders, on a regular basis, that you did not bear this child. One is not able to have discussions of physical similarities or comparisons to grandparents, aunts and uncles, siblings, etc. When you talk about your ancestry, there is a sensitivity required as your adopted child knows they have nothing in common with your biological ancestors.

Even emotional and personality characteristics, talents and habits, and mental ability come into play when considering the adjustment of the adopted child in the family. These are all sensitive issues that remind the parents, again and again, that they did not give birth to this child and remind the child as she's growing up that she does not have a biological connection to her adoptive parents. The issues of genetics and heritage can be quite sensitive subjects to discuss with the adopted child as they reach adolescence and are forming their own personal identity. Even in an open adoption, the adoptee may have difficulty accepting the reasons for being taken from their biological family and raised in a family for which they have no genetic heritage. It may be necessary to access the help of a pastor or counselor to guide the adoptive parents and adoptee in the discussion of the circumstances of the adoption. Avoiding the subject and believing that it is not important can have lifelong, emotional adjustment consequences for the adoptee, the adoptive parents, and their relationship with the adoptee.

The Support System

Evaluating one's support system is important also in the process of considering adoption. The better the family support and church support systems, the better it is in raising any child but even more important with adoption. A loving and cohesive family with supportive aunts, uncles, cousins, etc., can help the adoptee adjust and become a bonded member of a family unit. A church family can also not only give the adoptee the emotional support of other adults but also many friends their own age with whom they can interact and build healthy relationships. Regular scriptural instruction can assist the adoptee in making a strong commitment to God, experience redemption through Jesus Christ, and establish the values needed for a successful life.

Not long after adopting our daughter, a little less than a year, we decided to travel with a gospel singing group, requiring living in a motor home. We and another couple were in our early thirties and the other couple had two young boys, our daughter's age, which was enjoyable for her. After almost a year, we returned to our home for a year and then sold our home and moved to another state to work with a home mission's church along with our pastor's family. They had children and we directed and taught in a preschool/kindergarten in which our daughter was enrolled. After two years, we believed we were to work with a large, evangelistic ministry in another state where we bought a home and remained for three years before returning home. During this time, our daughter was either homeschooled or attended a private Christian school. After returning home, our daughter attended two different private Christian schools and a couple of years at a public school. In retrospect, it had been a concern that these changes were too disruptive for her in that they interrupted family ties and made it difficult to establish long-term friendships with peers. A couple should evaluate whether their lifestyle or life decisions might negatively impact a child who has already experienced a great deal of change and instability. Our daughter related to us that it was a fun adventure for her to make some of these changes but, looking back, it may not have been particularly stabilizing for her.

The Sibling Question

Personally, when possible, adopt another child or children to provide a sibling(s) as siblings may help the adoptee form relationships and begin to learn to play and socialize in a positive, constructive manner. If one is able to adopt more than one child within a short period of time, an adoptee will have the opportunity to experience and develop social skills which will help both adoptees in relationship with others. It would also help them to see that they are not alone in their adoption experience. Some areas have adoption support groups where adoptive parents and adoptees can interact and establish helpful friendships.

Biological Family Connection

Establishing parameters for a relationship with the biological mother and family should be considered before the placement of a child in one's home. Open adoptions are the trend today and have been found to be more beneficial to the adoptee in understanding the circumstances of their adoption and understanding their heritage. Otherwise, children in a "closed" adoption, Jean Lifton says, "grow up feeling like anonymous people cut off from the genetic and social heritage that gives everyone else roots."[72] Jean Lifton explains,

> "In the closed adoption system, if you rear someone else's child, you tell him about how he entered your clan and very little about the clan from which he came. His identity is supposed to start from the moment he became part of your family, and he is expected to live as a child without a past."[73]

---

72. Lifton, *Journey to the Adopted Self,* 8.
73. Lifton, *Journey,* 38.

Is Adoption in the Plan?

Personally, thinking that we were protecting our adoptive daughter from a biological mother and family members with life adjustment issues, which might be damaging to her, we opted for a closed adoption. In hindsight and with further knowledge, it may have been much better for her to have had this family heritage connection and the opportunity to establish some relationship even in monitored form.

The personal connection with the biological mother and/or family may be arranged "open" or "semi-open," depending on the circumstances. Visits can be informal, family-oriented and independent, or more formal, supervised, and dependent on certain conditions for time and location. The private adoption agency or state adoption agency can assist in working out visitation arrangements that are best for the child.

Redemptive View of Adoption

For a Christian adoptive couple, viewing adoption as a part of God's overall adoption plan for all of us can give them a sense of connection and renewal that can be passed on to the adoptee. An adoptee can come to understand adoption through the eyes of a loving God who has created a plan from the beginning of time through His Son, Jesus Christ, to redeem all those who would receive Him. As Julie Smith Lowe puts it, "They need to develop a redemptive view of adoption, meaning that our own personal assurance, comfort, and hope come from the fact that we have a loving Creator/Father who takes our brokenness and the brokenness of this world and redeems it."[74] Their brokenness, with a constructive perspective which does not emphasize them as victims but rather as victors, can provide them with a platform to confront any challenge in life with strength. Apparent weaknesses can actually be turned into strengths that cannot be gained any other way. Knowing God has always had a plan for their life that can make them the person they were meant to be, not despite but because of the obstacles and difficulties they faced, can be reassuring. This can be a life-changing revelation not only for them but for others they may be able to help.

Adoption can be the most rewarding experience one can imagine, especially if the adoptive couple is prepared and have not set their expectations into the realm of some unrealistic notion. It can be an experience as close as possible to bearing a child, biologically. When bonds are formed, properly, there will be no difference in how one feels about an adopted child. When they grow up and have their own family and make the adoptive parents grandparents, one will rarely think about the lack of genetic connection. The love you pour into your family will reap rewards of a long-lasting, spiritual bond which cannot be severed.

---

74. Lowe, *Counseling the Adopted Child*, 42.

Is Adoption in the Plan?

Even though we look back and realize that we were not totally prepared, we feel confident that God planned for our adoption of our daughter. The story is still being told and will continue to impact us and her for our entire lives and beyond. We believe God will bring about His will for the complete redemption through Jesus Christ of all of our souls and the five grandchildren now a part of our lives. God is using the perfect and imperfect of our lives to bring us all closer to Him, now and for eternity.

Fortunately, there are now numerous books and articles covering the variety of emotional issues adoptive parents might face with an adopted child. These resources have become more prevalent since the 1980s when there were few studies and very little literature available for adoptive parents. The previous literature on adoption covered very little concerning the difficulties of transition for the adoptee that had been with a biological family or in a foster home prior to the adoption. The literature did not cover the emotional trauma the adoptive children and even infants were experiencing in trying to adapt to a foreign situation. Anyone considering adoption should study the issues of the emotional impact on these children and be prepared to address the issues in a loving way that might help them overcome the trauma they have experienced. A list of some recommended books on adoption is available in the appendix of this book. There are many other options available by searching online.

While considering whether adoption is appropriate for you and your husband, or is not, how you move forward is important, either way the decision goes. Discover how we were able to consider God's plan for our life in a way that made the future hopeful. Open the pages of chapter nine and begin to see hope for your future.

CHAPTER NINE

FACING THE FUTURE

After years of infertility research, unsuccessful treatments, and hours considering the options of accepting childlessness or considering adoption, the future now loomed before us as an infertile couple. We were joyful and thankful that we had been able to adopt successfully but we didn't know whether another adoption was possible. It looked unlikely that we would have a biological child even though I, especially, always held out that hope. Realistically, the journey had come to the point of finally accepting the outcome, being thankful for the daughter God had provided, and attempting to live peacefully with what the future now appeared to be.

Each couple's experience, at this point, contains a different set of circumstances in how they arrived at a decision. One couple may have come to the conclusion that adoption does not fit them or their lifestyle. They accept being childless. Another couple may have attempted to adopt but were unsuccessful or found that there was no adoptable child which fit what they could accept. Or, another couple may have been successful in adoption but still mourn in their hearts for a biological child. Especially for the woman, adoption can be fulfilling in many ways but it may be, as it was for me, that she still feels the pain of the loss of her biological motherhood.

For many women, the pain of losing biological motherhood, the inability to carry a baby and give birth, is an emotional pain that is difficult to accept but one they will have to learn to live with. Even if an adoption is successful this pain may still remain. As explained in the previous chapter, adoption can come with some challenging bonding issues which can affect the fulfillment of motherhood. These issues can not only affect the relationship during the years of raising the child but for years to come in how family bonding is either maintained or becomes strained. In whatever state the couple is, there is a somewhat different emotional perspective on how they will need to adjust to the future and their family as it is.

So, are you thinking, "Now what?" Are you at a point where you have generally accepted the loss of biological motherhood but are feeling unfulfilled in your life? At this point, I had to block out the lies I was listening to in my mind and remind myself that I still had something important to contribute to life, especially that could be passed on to future generations. It was important for me to grasp that each woman is much more than her ability to biologically procreate.

Women are each created by God with many unique talents and abilities in numerous areas from artistic gifts to leadership and people skills. Above all, they are the recipients of God's love through the gospel which when accepted can impact others for eternity more than any earthly skill or ability. There are numerous ways to live out the gospel and be a productive, creative, contributing, and fruitful woman. Regardless of my feelings of loss, I knew God had given us a special gift and we must do our very best to raise our special daughter to be a happy, caring person who loves and serves the Lord.

Fruitful Can Mean Different Things

While *fruitful* can mean "fertile," it can also mean "productive of good results; profitable,"[75] with synonyms such as, "generative, yielding, bountiful, and exuberant."[76] As every woman is blessed with gifts from God, each has special talents, personality characteristics, and ideas to contribute. Each is useful, worthwhile, beneficial, and valuable. God did not create a woman to be a mother with nothing else important to share. In fact, the years a woman may be

---

75. *The Random House College Dictionary*, s.v. "fertile."
76. Joseph Devlin, s.v. "fertile," *A Dictionary of Synonyms and Antonyms*, Popular Library Edition (New York, NY: Fawcett Popular Library, 1961).

given outside of motherhood are, potentially, greater in number than those in which she is directly and primarily a mother. Whether one has never given birth to a biological child, has lost a child through death, estrangement, failed adoption, or is an empty nester, life has many more opportunities to share one's talents. Besides, beyond sharing one's talents, becoming a spiritual mother or mentor and/or a giving friend who emotionally and spiritually supports others may be the most valuable.

Do not sell yourself short. Discover how much you are needed by your spouse, your nieces and nephews, parents, siblings, friends, your church, and community. There is so much heartache and loneliness in the world and not just in far-off lands but also in your own home, church, neighborhood, and community. Be the one who is always there, praying, supporting, encouraging, phoning, writing kind notes, and giving a helping hand. It will be surprising how much you are appreciated and what impact your efforts can make.

Children are one of many blessings of life and obviously a very necessary blessing to ensure the continuation of the human race. However, there are many other blessings and needed roles for people to play in life which are designed especially for each one and carry a great deal of importance in carrying out God's plan. Consequently, when it becomes obvious that bearing a child or even adopting a child

Facing the Future

is not possible, one must arrive at the conclusion and accept this is not the role in God's plan for their contribution to humankind. While bearing children seems to be an enviable role, there are other roles which are also rewarding, fruitful, and carry a great deal of importance in the scheme of things.

Express yourself with the talents and abilities God has given you. The time available not raising children may be time that can be used to develop a talent which will touch many lives. It may be a talent to write, paint, play a musical instrument, and create in numerous ways that will not only be enjoyable to you but also to thousands with whom your abilities are shared. Thankfully, the Lord has always instilled in me the desire to serve in some way in the church and community, as well as stay busy with creative endeavors. There is so much in the world to enjoy. I am left me with no room for boredom. I believe we should strive to be fruitful with every minute God has given and use those moments to their fullest potential. Do not think you have been given an empty basket but a basket that can reap a bountiful harvest of fruit to share.

It is normal to struggle, on one hand, recognizing and being thankful for the gift from God of talents and abilities while, on the other hand, feeling the right to bear children had been denied. Frankly, it may seem harsh but it became clear to me, from a biblical perspective, that we come into this world with no actual rights at all. The fact that you even exist at all is only by the will and grace of God. Personally, there have been several times since my own birth that illness or an accident could have ended my life. One can only deduct that there must have been a reason for me surviving and be grateful for the opportunity to continue to share one's God-given abilities with others in this life. Whatever you receive in talents and blessings is from the hand of God. That which God determines to be a blessing designed for you is totally within His control.

Do not underestimate God's purpose in working through women with various roles, talents, and abilities. Some women are called to a position within teaching, writing, medicine, missionary work, charity work, music, or other areas within their talent or ability which require tremendous devotion. Meeting the expectations of time and devotion to perfect a skill or ability leaves little time to also be a mother. Some have done both and have been successful but the strain can be monumental, unless they have been given supernatural ability to balance both roles. Some couples pursue complementary roles that are fulfilling for both and contribute a great deal to other people. However, while children have been a blessing even in these situations, children certainly require special attention for which the burden falls primarily on the woman. That is not to say, however, a couple should deliberately choose not to bear children so they may pursue a role in their talent or abilities; but, if they are not able to bear children, they will certainly be more free to focus on the role in which God has placed them. Also, they will have the time to enjoy each other in the process.

For instance, why do many parents look forward to being empty nesters? They look forward to a time when they can enjoy each other without the constant need to nurture, direct, and worry about a house full of children struggling to grow into mature, contributing adults. Of course there is much to enjoy along the way in raising a family and looking forward to grandchildren. However, there is also much to be said about time to appreciate each other and some activities and enjoyable times alone.

There are always those seemingly perfect families where everything seems to be wonderful and hum along with little difficulty. It is more likely that many families have some troubling stories along the way, some that are heartbreaking. Do not covet the life of others as you might find out why it was not the life God planned for you and your particular personality.

It may still be difficult for many to see the benefit and value in being childless. It may seem like one has won the consolation prize while hoping for a blue ribbon. Truly, it may seem so if one feels like all their hopes and dreams have been shattered. However, just like in any loss, there is another opportunity, a silver lining, which one may not be able to see at first. If one refuses to give up but instead looks for opportunity and other doors of possibility, the answer will come, the door will open. Life can be rich and full when one is able to see the joy and fulfillment in areas one never dreamed might be in God's design. When you get past the hurt and pain of the loss, the vibrant colors of life will become clearer. Life can bring on new meaning as one listens for God's voice and the guidance of the Holy Spirit showing where most of the needs are. This does not necessarily mean that God has some highly visible or exalted position or role in mind. It may be one in the background, in a supportive role rather than in a leadership role. Whatever the role is, embrace it with joy as God's plan. Carry it out to the best of your ability, giving God the glory for creating and designing what He called you to do in His sovereign will.

God Has a Plan for Your Life

If one believes in the sovereign will of God, one must come to the conclusion that the loss of motherhood or, at least, child bearing is in God's plan for their life. Somehow, this loss fits into God's overall, sovereign plan for the world and universe. That may sound outlandish and incredible, but in the Bible, the Lord says, "My ways are higher than your ways" (Isaiah 55:9b, English Standard Version). He knows when the sparrow falls and He numbers every hair on our heads (Matthew 10:29 and Luke 12:7). Within the truth of those Scriptures is an incredible thought. Since He numbers the very hairs on my head, I must conclude that He loves and cares about who I am, what I need, and how He plans to use my life for His glory in my corner of the world. Somehow, beyond our comprehension, it all fits together in one glorious plan of redemption for me and all mankind. Consequently, I must believe that my loss of childbearing is part of His plan and that He loves me with all the compassion and care that He loves anyone.

Our ideas of what life for us should look like is influenced so deeply by family traditions, societal traditions, customs, culture, trends, politics, media, music, literature, poetry, and philosophy. Many of the concepts of life and culture have nothing to do with God or His principles and plan set forth in His biblical word. Developing a concept of life from man's perspective will leave one totally confused and off-track for what is actually intended for one's life. Only God knows His plan for each one's life and it does not include mankind's idea of what is important.

Desiring a child certainly seems like it should fit into God's plan as bearing children was encouraged and highly honored in the Bible. Obviously, God wanted to share His love with many people and wanted them to receive that love in worship and service. Actually, the vast majority of people throughout biblical times and throughout history have not loved and served God. However, whether they serve Him or not, God has given people a natural desire to want children and raise them to be successful. Each child is a precious and beautiful gift, a reminder of the wonder of God's creation.

Many couples have a desire to nurture and care for an innocent child. When there is no child of one's own to nurture, it seems something is missing that still desires to be expressed and experienced. We were thankful to be able to raise a daughter but desired to adopt another child. Unfortunately, this did not come about for various reasons. We came to accept that there was a reason for us to raise only this one special child. However, we realized raising a child was not the only way a nurturing desire can be expressed? Just because the desire to bear or raise a child seems natural to all of us, does not mean it is right for all of us or part of God's plan for each life.

We all fit into God's plan for His kingdom, whether or not we love and serve Him. What our individual purpose is can only be fully known by God. Our highest, individual purpose is to love, worship, and serve God. To carry out this purpose, one must strive to know God through the word He has provided and the daily guidance of the Holy Spirit. It is our purpose to build a relationship with God by understanding as much as possible about His love for us in providing a relationship with Him through His Son, Jesus Christ. There is no greater aim in life. Everything else we experience in life should be an expression of our love for Him and gratitude for His plan of salvation. Whether it is our occupation, hobby, family relations, daily tasks of living, or communication with and assistance to others should all be an expression of God working in our lives and carrying out His plan. "You are not your own for you were bought with a price" (1 Corinthians 6:19–20, English Standard Version). It is not doing every day "what we love to do" but how we express what we do every day in glorification of God. Once we get our focus off of ourselves and focus on knowing God and glorifying Him, life has a different meaning.

Life can be more about enjoying God's plan. The stress of trying to make one's life what one thinks it should be can be overwhelming. Life rarely follows our plan and has many surprising twists and turns. When one is able to relax and let God direct their path, one can trust God and be satisfied with the plan God has designed for their life.

Live in the Hope of God Carrying Out His Perfect Plan in Your Life

What is the goal of life? The Bible clearly states the goal is to love and glorify God. In every activity or task, the purpose should be to love and glorify God. Many times, the goal and purpose is ignored as self-focus tends to be the norm. Personal goals and desires can get in the way of the true goal of life as agendas and desires are set without regard for God's plan. That is not to say that God has no understanding or care for the personal life and desires of the individual. The Bible clearly indicates that God greatly loves and cares for each one.

The greatest example of His love is the sacrifice of His Son on the cross which is greater than any gift one could receive. Without Jesus Christ, one's personal desires and plans are futile, anyway. All is lost and useless without the saving grace provided through Jesus Christ. Without Jesus Christ, we are lost souls wandering the earth for a short period of time, making an attempt to eke out some happiness in a world that seems often on a road to destruction.

Lining up one's life with God's plan can only bring satisfaction and happiness. The more one grasps that God chose a plan for their life that fits into His overall plan for humankind one can realize a greater sense of acceptance and satisfaction. Knowing God in a more intimate way through prayer, reading, studying His Word, and walking with Him through daily tasks will keep the focus off self-centered ideas and on those which glorify God and His plan.

For the believer, there is nothing more important than understanding that God loves you and has a plan for goodness and what will benefit you. It bears repeating, "For I know the plans I have for you, declares the Lord, plans for welfare and not for evil, to give you a future and a hope" (Jeremiah 29:11, English Standard Version). It may appear that there is not anything good that can come out of being childless, but one must think beyond the human plane and seek the mind of God. This seems to be a somewhat impossible task in that there are those areas in the mind of God that must remain a mystery. However, the word of God does give us all we need to guide us in understanding how a seemingly horrible physical limitation might still be God's good plan for a person and part of His overall plan.

Firstly, God's Word and actions in Scripture do make it clear that He is concerned about each individual. However, it is also clear that God has a plan that is wide in scope and encompasses all of humankind. Each one of us fits into that plan in some miraculous way. Even those who never come to know God are still a part of His plan. For the believer, God is certainly working out His plan. The believer is not alone, adrift without a rudder. God wants one's attention focused on Him for His glory, not for what one might think is their personal plan. He will remind those who listen to His voice on a day-to-day basis where He wants their focus and sometimes will reveal the impact one is having on others through the influence of His Holy Spirit. Much of the time, though, it may be difficult to see how one's individual life is impacting others and how it fits into a part of His plan but one must trust that it is.

Secondly, who are we to judge the will of God for each of us, individually or as a body of believers? He is in control and it is our duty before Him to act righteously and glorify Him in our actions. We are not to question the circumstances of our life, whether we are rich or poor, where we are born, our nationality, the color of our skin, our physical looks, or physical abilities or limitations. We are not to covet the material things of others or the life circumstances which may appear to be better than our own. One must trust God that the life one has been given is the perfect fit.

Each of us has a purpose in God's kingdom. It is not for us to decide how that purpose will be brought forth in the scheme of everything and played out in our lives. One may try to manipulate the path and goals of life but, in the end, God's will is done regardless of how much one tries to change certain aspects. Life happens in ways one does not expect. There are surprises at every turn. Some seem wonderful and beautiful and others seem like horrible blows to what one would expect. The wonderful and beautiful as well as the losses and disappointments are all a part of the plan of God for humankind. Does this seem harsh and difficult to grasp? God knows people do not want to accept His ways but He says that all of it will work for His glory and for good. Trust Him through the grief and sorrow. Live in joy, accepting the path that has been chosen. As Paul said, "commending ourselves as servants of God" .

. . "as sorrowful yet always rejoicing" (2 Corinthians 6:4a and 6:10a).

How Does One Trust God?

When one's life seems to be going forward in a positive path with little trouble or adversity, it is easy to trust God and believe His goodness is being bestowed on us. The Bible speaks in many passages about the goodness, love, and compassion of God. However, when adversity comes our way and there does not seem to be an answer and the struggle or trial continues for months and years, one begins to have moments of doubt in God's goodness. Desiring a child yet being childless is a long and painful ordeal with reminders at every turn along the path. It can easily become the overarching pursuit of a couple's life and draw their attention away from the daily blessings and goodness of God.

One might ask themselves if their focus on this one desire, the desire to give birth to and raise a child, is blinding them to the great blessings, gifts, talents, and ministry opportunities God has called them to. One scratch or nick, even a tiny paper cut, can draw one's entire attention to the point of not being able to think about anything else. However, when we change our focus and get involved with someone else's need or get busy with a task, soon, we forget about that pain and often do not notice until much later that it has gone away. Obviously, the pain of being childless is a much larger pain, but the same comparison can be made to the smaller pains in life.

It's a matter of focus and being willing to be open and trusting of a God who has a plan for us much greater than what we have imagined and which fits into His overall plan for humankind. We may never know completely why we have had to endure this particular pain, but we must trust that there is a reason far greater than can be seen or understood. It is possible to be satisfied with being childless and even be completely happy and content with the life God has chosen.

How does one find satisfaction in life? First, trust God and then change the focus of one's attention. Much of our dissatisfaction is centered in a self-focus approach to life and our daily tasks and plans and not in what God is guiding us to do. The Bible says, "and having done all, to then stand firm" (Ephesians 6:13b, English Standard Version). This means that after one has followed the Lord's instruction in putting on the "whole armor of God," then one should trust the Lord to carry out His purpose in one's life with the guidance of the Holy Spirit. Direct one's attention to others as one walks in faith and carries forward the gospel in whatever way the Lord guides. Do not get bogged down in self-focus but stand firm in faith in the gospel and be prepared to act as guided. "The people who know their God shall stand firm and take action" (Daniel 11:32b, English Standard Version).

Facing the Future

Even with trusting God, is it all right to mourn for what seems like a lost joy in life? Does the Lord understand the suffering of those who cannot bear children? Does the Lord understand sorrow and grief? Is consolation to be found in the comfort of the Lord? Yes, of course. Those may seem like totally unnecessary questions but ones the childless woman often asks. But God knows the pain and sorrow one goes through in many life situations. Jesus Christ walked in the footsteps of man through every possible pain, insult, lost friends, sorrow over hurting, rebellious people, and a torturous death. He was moved by the death of Lazarus, had sorrow for Lazarus' family and friends, and wept (John 11:33–35). He was sorrowful over Jerusalem and wept over His people who would not listen (Luke 19:41–42). He saw and experienced how people hurt in life and He experienced the worst of it, yet He continued to glorify His Father and follow the plan for His life.

God did not promise that life would be easy as the fall of man brought much pain and suffering, but He did and does promise to be with us through all our hurts and losses. David cried out to God in distress over enemies. Anyone in desperate sorrow can relate to his words when he said, "Be gracious to me, O Lord, for I am in distress; my eye is wasted away from grief, my soul and my body also. For my life is spent with sorrow, and my years with sighing" (Psalm 31:9–10). At the end of his sorrow, he rose up with confidence as he said, "Be strong, and let your heart take courage, all you who hope in the Lord" (Psalm 31:24). The Lord Jesus said, "I will never desert you, nor will I ever forsake you" (Hebrews 13:5). He has kept His promises and will continue to keep His promises throughout the life of those who seek and follow Him.

In studying the life of Christ, one can see His great compassion and sorrow for humankind. Jesus Christ grieved over Jerusalem because the Jewish leadership and many people refused to accept Him and the gospel. He had understanding and compassion for grieving mothers and parents of children who were sick or who had died. He grieved for a friend who had died. Most of all, he grieved for those who would not listen and were blind to their sin and spiritual condition. Jesus was "a man of sorrows and acquainted with grief" (Isaiah 53:3a). He understood suffering and loss but had compassion on the multitudes and gave them hope. He said, "Blessed are those who mourn, for they shall be comforted" (Matthew 5:4).

Mourning over loss may take some time and will be unique for each woman's experience with infertility. One's loss might include no pregnancies, miscarriages, failed adoptions, or the death of a child, leaving one without the ability to conceive again. Grief from these losses can be ongoing over the years, especially with each loss or disappointment, but also felt strongly as the childbearing years come to a

Facing the Future

close. Recovery can be a roller coaster. Zimmerman points out, "Like all grief, it is impossible to tell how long it will take to recover from this particular loss or what exactly will help."[77] One must take some time to transition into a life one did not expect.

The expectation of a life with a family of children and grandchildren has obviously been altered. At this point, decisions have to be made so as not to get bogged down in a depressive state, unable to see the plan of God for one's life. Possibly, one has become disillusioned with God and it is difficult to trust Him. You may think God has been deserting you all along and certainly will not be here for you when your life needs a new direction. However, through a time of mourning, one must trust the promises of God which have been there all along. Welch clarifies this point when he says,

> If you think God is far away and indifferent, here is the surprising revelation. From the foundation of the world, God knew your sufferings and declared that he himself would take human form and participate in them (which means that we too could share in his). This is not a distant, indifferent God.[78]

---

77. Zimmerman, *A Spiritual Companion to Infertility*, 140.
78. Welch, *Depression*, 48.

The story of Rachel in the Book of Genesis of the Bible is an example of a woman who became obsessed with childbearing. The desire to bear children became an idol and eventually destroyed her. Rachel was beautiful and beloved by her husband, Jacob. However, Rachel was jealous of her sister Leah's fertility which brought Jacob several sons by Leah. Rachel begged her husband, Jacob, for a child, "Give me children, or else I die" (Genesis 30:1). It is interesting that she did not appear to seek God for her plight but took things into her own hands giving Jacob her maid, Bilhah, to bear children for her. She did give God credit for these births but her concern was more with her vindication from the shame and reproach she felt for not being able to bear children. Thankfully, God did answer her plea with the birth of Joseph. However, Rachel immediately begged for another child. She was not satisfied with the birth of a son. She seemed more concerned with her own reputation, "God has taken away my reproach" (Genesis 30:23). In giving birth to her second child, Ben-Oni (child of my sorrow, later changed to Benjamin), she "suffered severe labor" and died (Genesis 35:16-18).

The story of Rachel is sad. Rachel believed she was entitled in many ways. Not only did she believe God must give her children, she also believed she had been cut short of her inheritance (Genesis 31:14). Even though she was highly desired and loved, these were not enough for her. Jacob had wisely, with God's

Facing the Future

guidance, built massive wealth in livestock and could provide anything Rachel needed but she still found it necessary to steal her father's idols. Idol worship was obviously a family custom. It is not surprising that Rachel could turn any concern or focus into an idol as this was a custom to which she was comfortable and must have believed would bring her the desired result. It was not common for her to trust the one true God with His purpose for her life. She could have been experiencing much more happiness if she would have been patient. Rachel could have enjoyed Leah's children and could have been an emotional support to Leah considering Leah was not well-loved like she. Instead, she was actually selfish and self-centered, ignoring or overlooking a great opportunity to minister to Leah. She could have also appreciated the love of Jacob more, praising God for her favored status.

Focus with gratitude on the great benefits and talents God has given which can be a tremendous blessing to others. Take joy in all the activities one finds enjoyable, both great and small, which bring satisfaction not only individually but to others. Make the most of what God has given and redirect one's attention to those things. If a person has already developed God-given talents and abilities and has used them in benefitting others, then that person is far ahead in preparation to accept His plan for their life.

Trust God that not only can you be satisfied and content in this life but also, possibly more importantly, the experience of being childless can be used to touch the lives of others who are childless or are grieving with a similar loss. Walking successfully through grief and loss prepares one for overcoming many trials in life. Arm yourself with the promises of God and be prepared to live life fully in trust and contentment, sharing the love of God with a hurting world.

In learning to trust God with His plan for my life, I was able to find satisfaction and true joy in what God had provided and in sharing my gifts with others. The joy I was missing became more fully realized as I learned to appreciate the gifts and blessings He had already given in a saving grace through Jesus Christ. I also came to realize more fully how my gifts and experiences could be used to help others. Chapter ten provides suggestions for how the loss and mourning of infertility can be turned into the joy of sharing. Turn to chapter ten for the overcoming conclusion of how joy can come out of what seems like a tragedy.

CHAPTER TEN

DANCING WITH JOY TO SHARE

Is it possible to appreciate the joy of others mothering children, help them with mothering, and still have complete joy in your home and your heart? The Lord promises us this joy without qualification as we abide in Him. He cares about each one of us just the way we are. The physical differences we see as imperfections are not such to the Lord. We are not perfect in the way He intended before the Fall, but we are perfectly fitted for His glory in His strength and purpose because we are in Christ. The Lord told Paul, "My grace is sufficient for you, for power is perfected in weakness" (2 Corinthians 12:9a). Many have biological limits but God did not create them to punish them or make their lives miserable. He has a plan for each one and promises joy and contentment regardless of the limitations one has to experience.

Pathway to Peace and Joy beyond Infertility

Joni Eareckson Tada is an incredible example of a life recreated to exemplify talents and gifts despite limitations, pain, and suffering.

> He has a plan and purpose for my time on earth. He is the master artist or sculptor, and He is the one who chooses the tools He will use to perfect His workmanship. What of suffering, then? What of illness? What of disability? Am I to tell Him which tools He can use and which tools He can't use in the lifelong task of perfecting me and molding me into the beautiful image of Jesus?[79]

True, it is natural and good to desire children to raise and bless our home, but it is not the be-all and end-all to a beautiful life of walking with the Lord and experiencing the goodness and joy of life. James says, "Consider it all joy," as one encounters the trials, tribulations, and disappointments of life as these are the testing of our faith giving one endurance to move forward to full perfection and completion in Christ Jesus (James 1:2–4).

"He makes the barren woman abide in the house, as a joyful mother of children. Praise the Lord!" This verse, Psalm 113:9, speaks of the promise of joy. The

---

79. Tada, *A Place of Healing*, 66.

Dancing with Joy to Share

psalmist is referring to Hannah's answered prayer. However, even though the psalmist is referring to a woman living in a home with the joy of children, the Scripture also speaks about joy over the redemption of souls. Psalms 113–118 were sung at the end of the Passover meal as part of the Hallel and then possibly sang by Jesus and His apostles at the Last Supper in praise to God for condescending down to the lowly.[80] The Lord loves the barren woman and desires to give her joy in her relationship with Him and in her work in planting seeds to bring children into the kingdom of God. John Boys, Dean of Canterbury and author, gives great credence to works of faith beyond rearing children when he says:

> Our chief joy on this earth is found in our relationship with Christ our Savior. Children are a joy and a treasure but our primary goal is to store up treasures in heaven (Matthew 6:20). Or it may be construed of true Christians: all of us are by nature barren of goodness, conceived and born in sin, not able to think a good thought (2 Corinthians 3:5); but the Father of lights and mercies makes us fruitful and abundant always in the work of the Lord (1 Corinthians 15:58); he giveth us grace to be fathers and

---

80. William Smith, *Smith's Bible Dictionary*, rev. ed. (Nashville, TN: Holman Bible Publishers, 1979), 121.

mothers of many good deeds, which are our children and best heirs, eternizing our name forever.[81]

The spiritual joy of a barren woman can bring joy to her home, to her husband, and to all who enter therein. A barren woman with a joyful spirit in the Lord can bring forth spiritual children as she lives out God's purpose in her life and those she touches. "As a joyful mother" could be interpreted as "just like" a "mother of children." The barren woman's joy may be just as complete as she lives out God's will in her life and finds contentment in doing so. The Lord not only promises joy but uses strong, definite, forceful terms to show that He will carry out His promise by making the barren woman dwell in an atmosphere of joy. Steven Cole instructs well by saying, "Cry out to Him in your spiritual barrenness to fill you with His joy. In your weakness, rely on His strength."[82]

Another one of my favorite portions of Scripture related to Psalm 113:9 is Isaiah 54:1. "Shout for joy, O barren one, you who have borne no child." Even though Isaiah 54:1 is speaking of the restoration of God's chosen people after their suffering in Babylon,

---

81. John Boys, Exposition of Psalm 113:9, Works of John Boys, Explanatory Notes and Quaint Sayings, 846–861, Bible Study Tools, accessed September 16, 2019, http://www. Biblestudytools.com/commentaries/treasury-of-david/psalms-113:9.html.
82. Steven J. Cole, "Psalm 113: God Is Great and He Is Gracious," Bible.org, accessed September 17, 2019, https://www.bible.or/seriespage/psalm113-god-great-and-he-gracious.

it is interesting that He compares their plight to that of a woman who has "borne no child." He speaks of their desolation and state of despair as one would imagine a childless wife, or a widow who was left alone without any children to comfort her or give her purpose. Even though the Hebrew people at this time are a meager, humiliated number with few earthly goods, God is promising them restoration. The restoration He speaks of is not in their physical numbers or earthly glory since these rewards are far below what He really intended. God's primary purpose was the redemption of their souls through their cleansing from the idol-worshipping culture from which they had emerged. The increase of their spiritual number by true, heart-changing experiences gave the angels a reason to rejoice and a reason for Hebrew people to shout for joy that their God had not abandoned them and, above all else, cared about an exclusive relationship with them.

For the childless woman who feels abandoned by God, Isaiah 54:1 should be an encouragement and give her strength of purpose. It speaks to me of the importance of bearing spiritual children when the Lord says, "The sons of the desolate one will be more numerous than the sons of the married woman." God is much more concerned with the gospel being spread to all who will hear and His kingdom expanding with spiritual children. Many will give birth to biological children, some of whom will serve the Lord and some will not. Some will listen but for whatever reason will not respond to the gospel presented to them. Some will never respond. But for those who may still respond or have never yet heard, the harvest is waiting for someone God has called to reap the harvest of their souls and bring them forth as spiritual children for the kingdom of God. Shout for joy that you may be the one to bear more spiritual children than you ever could have biologically.

I was encouraged by realizing that my purpose on earth is much more meaningful than bearing biological children and passing on my genes to the next generation. It is not for us to know how many more generations will be generated before the Lord's return. The real issue is how many of those generations will turn to the Lord and pass on the only vital, life-giving message, the gospel of Jesus Christ. Be encouraged that you can be one of the most important life-givers of all, a spiritual mother.

It has become important for me to grasp and emphasize to other childless or infertile women and/or couples how important spiritual children are in the kingdom of God. Life in the spiritual sense is not about biological children. The goal in life is not about what we can achieve in the flesh. Paul pointedly stated, "But whatever things were gain to me, those things I have counted as loss for the sake of Christ" (Philippians 3:7). Thousands need spiritual mentoring from a big brother, sister, or parent figure. We need to think beyond the physical realm and see life as a spiritual walk in the Lord who orders every step of the believer to carry out His plan of redemption for humanity. Not only is every personal contact we make important but also those made through social media or in other correspondence within one's circle of friends and acquaintances. A believer's role is to be light and salt to the world regardless of whether your world contains biological children, spiritual children, or both. Anyone can be a spiritual child whether they are young or old in physical years. Everyone, regardless of their position of understanding or level of spiritual need, can benefit from the love and compassion of another believer who can assist them in focusing on the great and mighty promises in God's Word.

Becoming a Spiritual Mother

How can you be a spiritual mother? First of all, nurture a heart for lost souls. Study the Scriptures that speak of Jesus' compassion and that of His disciples for the lost. Look around you in your family, church, and community and a vast number of opportunities will appear. See their hurting hearts. Some are vocal about their struggles whether with relationships, life's trials, or health concerns, but others will be very discreet. Press in and let them know you care and are willing to listen. Show compassion and care in all contacts with people. Obviously, people take time. If there is little time to spend in a lengthy relationship with one who is hurting, let them know you still care and will be supportive in their time of need. Prepare in prayer and knowledge of the Scriptures in order to provide the guidance needed or point one to a biblical counselor. Early in any relationship, the first goal is to show compassion, care, and nurture a trusting relationship.

Study the Scriptures, especially pertaining to presenting the gospel. There are a number of Scripture study guides and complementary books by excellent authors which will help in preparation or are helpful to give to those in need. Develop a handy reference tool of salvation gospel Scriptures and comforting words from the Bible. Keep a guide in your purse and at home so you will always be prepared. "Show yourself approved" by being ready for any opportunity that arises to share the gospel. Write out a simple, personal testimony in how Jesus Christ has impacted and is impacting your life. People want to know what the gospel of Christ means to you, personally.

Get involved in your church and community. If teaching does not seem to be your calling, just get involved in volunteering in order to develop relationships with other people. Give of yourself in time and share your thoughts and everyday experiences. Develop relationships and trust with others. Let the Holy Spirit guide you as to the right time to share the gospel. Be sensitive to the needs of others and what may be the best timing for them. Heed the voice of the Holy Spirit concerning timing. Otherwise, you may push people away and there may not be an opening to the gospel again for a long time. Be sensitive to what the other person wants to talk about. One may be able to steer the conversation somewhat, especially if it is not a healthy subject matter, but do not take over the conversation. Do not jump into the conversation with personal hurts, struggles, and life experiences, unless the other person desires to hear your personal experience and it may be helpful to them. They want a listening ear, not a chatterbox, self-focused on personal experiences.

If you have the emotional and physical strength, do not be afraid to work with children whether in church, school, or other avenue of ministry. Thousands of children need a loving guide and touch. Thousands of children in our schools and in foster care do not have a caring adult capable of giving them the love they need. There are numerous opportunities where you can soften their hearts with love and, if allowed, share the gospel with them. Sharing love will be a gospel message to them even if one is not allowed to relate the gospel and Bible stories to them. Many public schools allow release time for the Good News Club Storytime trailers where one can volunteer to teach. If fostering children in the home is not a possibility, there are always incredible opportunities to provide for the needs of foster children and assist foster parents in their efforts.

Consider the talents the Lord has given and begin expressing those in areas of work and volunteerism. The Holy Spirit will guide in opening doors of opportunity wherever it is appropriate and fits into the Lord's individual plan for each one's life. Personally, I have found working as a Patient and Reproductive Grief Advocate volunteer at a local pregnancy clinic is a fulfilling way to be available to women making difficult decisions regarding their pregnancy, for those grieving infertility, or for the loss of an infant through miscarriage or stillbirth. The bottom line is that each one has a definite and fulfilling purpose regardless of the inability to bear children. Do not give up on what is surely your God-given role in the world. Be confident in knowing how much you are loved and needed in the scheme of God's plan. Bearing children is beautiful and important, but it is not the ultimate goal of life or the end-all purpose for every woman. Enjoy being a beautiful woman God created for much more and to be expressed in numerous ways for His glory. Your purpose above all else is to worship God, trust Him, and glorify Him in all you do.

Helping Other Childless Women

Childless women are all about us. They are the quiet ones in the conversations about the antics and

Dancing with Joy to Share

accomplishments of children and grandchildren. One does not have to look far to find a childless woman who may need the support of one who understands. Be aware of childless women and ask the Holy Spirit to direct you in sharing what you understand about infertility and the childless woman experience, being careful for the right time and the most sensitive way. Suggest a time to get together to talk over coffee or in a more in-depth, longer-term conversation. If the woman is a believer in Christ, one has an opportunity to assist her in exploring the love of God and His perfect plan for her. If she is an unbeliever, one has a great opportunity to be a friend and, when prompted by the Holy Spirit, to offer her God's eternal plan for her life in the gospel of Jesus Christ. She may be in the beginning of her journey to seek help for infertility or possibly coming to the end of her journey but still not content in God's plan for her life. A woman who has traveled this path and has come to the point of contentment and joyful acceptance of God's plan can be an incredible support and resource for those still finding their way.

Be careful with whom you share the details of your own experience. Once you discover who is childless in your circle, listen to determine if their experience might have some similarities. If so, carefully and privately, approach this woman. If there is common ground, it may be helpful and healing for both of you to discuss the difficulties and what you each discovered about how the Lord helped through your experiences. The other childless woman might be struggling more than you and need encouragement and a listening ear. Be sensitive and a good listener and you may find a mutually beneficial relationship of strength and encouragement.

Everyone has had a different experience. Many factors in your own life experience will make a difference in your relationship with other childless women. One's attitude toward childbearing, degree of the sense of loss, whether you adopted or not, how successful your adoption experience was, other areas of fulfillment in your life, your Christian walk, and other factors, make a difference in how you will relate to others in discussing infertility and childlessness. When you talk with other childless women, listen with compassion and interest and do not begin right away telling them about your own experience. Even though there are similarities that can be of benefit, their experience may be much different from your own. This does not mean you should not share your experience with other women. Just do not be surprised when there is little interest initially in what you have been through. Be sensitive. Some childless women might just need a listening ear. Some will find what you have been through helpful and may ask questions. Others are not ready to share or listen at all as they have already moved on and they do not care to discuss it further.

Dancing with Joy to Share

One always hears how those who have experienced a disability or have overcome a trial in their life are much better at empathizing and helping those who are going through something similar. Anyone with a compassionate heart can be a help to one who is trying to accept a disability, setback, or trial in their life. However, the deep commonality of one who has walked the path of a particular adversity or physical limitation cannot be replaced. What a childless, infertile woman who has desired biological children has experienced in pain and heartache cannot be compared in the depth of understanding and emotion needed in relating to other childless women. This unique understanding is valuable for those struggling with acceptance and needing to know how to move into God's perfect plan for them. What one has learned through an experience as a childless woman is tremendously valuable to other childless women.

The infertile, childless woman has much to share, not only from their own walk through childlessness but also in knowledge gained by researching the subject in medical literature and through Scripture. Drawing from experience, knowledge, and Scripture will allow one to be a well-rounded, supportive advocate of great benefit to other women trying to navigate the path of acceptance. Being well-rounded is important in that one may find that the struggling, childless woman who needs help has never talked with anyone else before about the subject outside of their husband. Only another prepared childless woman will ever be able to fully understand the path she has walked and be able to discuss the entire range of issues with her. Husbands can be compassionate and have certainly walked the path with their wives, but there are some pains and disappointments only another woman can understand. Of course, directing her to the Lord who understands all our pains, hurts, and disappointments is crucial but He also uses each of us to comfort and support each other. It is entirely true for us today as Paul told the Corinthians:

> Blessed be the God and Father of our Lord Jesus Christ, the Father of mercies and God of all comfort; who comforts us in all our affliction so that we may be able to comfort those who are in any affliction with the comfort with which we ourselves are comforted by God. (2 Corinthians 1:3–4)

Everyone's experience is unique. Do not say to the other childless woman, "I know what you have been through." It may be better to say, "I can relate to your experience because I see some similarities" or "I think I understand, but tell me what it has been like for you." Let the other woman talk about their experience and feelings without interrupting, except only where you find it particularly important and beneficial to her. Build a relationship of trust and friendship if the other woman is open to it. If they ask you for guidance, tell them what has been helpful for you in accepting childlessness. There may be Scriptures you can offer, a special book, or, if desired, in-depth counseling through the church or recommended counseling service. Mostly, be a friend who cares because you have a unique understanding of their pain and may be able to be an instrument of the Lord in helping them move beyond the sadness and mourning to a life of joy and meaning.

One does not have to be a trained counselor to offer support and a word of love and compassion. In the Scripture, one finds tremendous guidance far beyond anything a woman could receive from a counseling service, unless it is a Bible-focused counseling service. Point the childless woman to Scripture and point out the Scriptures which describe the great and wonderful compassion of God and desire for us to be content and at peace in Him. Explain how our greatest purpose is to glorify God and that He has promised us great rewards for our life here and eternally. His promises are for those with children and those who are childless. He makes no distinction. Yes, He says that one is blessed with a "quiver full" of children, but does not deny blessings and contentment for those who might have an empty quiver.

Helping the Church Family Understand

There are few people in the church family who will understand the experience of the infertile, childless couple or woman. They may show empathy and compassion but, for the most part, my experience is that they will hardly notice your pain. When a childless woman is a part of women's activities in the church, few will consider that their conversation might be uncomfortable for her. Talk of babies and childbirth and the difficulties of raising children are topics a childless woman may not feel comfortable participating in.

The lack of understanding in the church is not totally the fault of the church pastorate or lay family. Women are often uncomfortable talking about their infertility even around other women for various reasons which have been discussed. Their stigma, disappointment, and feelings of being different often cause them to avoid the subject. However, the childless woman can assist women in the church to be aware and understand by boldly educating them on the topic. Possibly a women's gathering topic might include the subject of infertility and the struggles of the infertile, childless woman. Instead of ignoring the subject, women in the church family should welcome knowledge and understanding on the subject. The childless woman should not expect other women to fully understand, but she should be willing to reach out to them to offer assistance in understanding.

Present the topic of infertility to the pastor, elders, or whoever is in charge of women's ministries in the church.

Community women's groups may also benefit from learning about infertility and the struggle of a childless woman or couple. If one has the confidence to speak to a community group, there may be an opportunity to bring encouragement to those who are struggling or need support to move forward in their life. Infertility clinics and health clinics may know of support groups or women's organizations that would be interested in the topic of infertility.

Chosen to Run a Race

Believers and followers of Christ have been chosen to run a race for the glory of God. How one's faith and trust in God is applied every day to this race determines the outcome. At the end of the race, what do we want to hear? "Well done, good and faithful servant" or "Welcome, you made it but your reward is small." Personally, I believe we have all been chosen for a position and purpose in the furtherance of the gospel which is part of a divine plan. Do not weigh your position and purpose as less than the best. Do not judge your position and purpose compared to someone else's. When you see other couples with their families and grandkids, do not be jealous and spend time wishing that was your family. Rejoice in what the Lord has given them as their position and purpose, but do not count it as greater in the overall plan of God. They may enjoy their children but you do not know the stress and difficulties they may have to face in their family. I trust God that He has me exactly where He wants me for His purpose and glory and not for my own particular joy and contentment. He is compassionate and cares about our joy, but our interpretation of joy and His are not the same. Seek His concept of true joy, peace, and contentment, not your own ideas which are skewed by the world and culture in which we live.

Paul suffered with pain from a physical condition which he asked God to take away (2 Corinthians 12:7). However, the pain and suffering from this condition was not relieved. Paul did not understand the reason for the pain. However, he was able to keep his focus on the calling of God for his life and did not let this painful condition thwart his efforts on a daily basis or become a roadblock to the overall race he was running. His goal was to carry out God's purpose and plan in his life and run the race well to the very end. He completed his goal and, from his words, it was evident that he was satisfied and pleased with the race he had run for the furtherance of the kingdom of God. Paul said, "I have fought the good fight, I have finished the course, I have kept the faith; in the future there is laid up for me the crown of righteousness, which the Lord, the righteous Judge, will award to me on that day; but also to all who have loved His appearing" (2 Timothy 4:7–8).

    If you are a follower of Christ, the Lord has already given you the greatest and most wonderful gift you could possibly receive in redemption from sin and eternal life with complete joy and peace forevermore. Anything a believer receives in this earthly life in the way of blessings, contentment, and material goods is like "frosting on the cake" in comparison. Time slips away every day, time in which one can enjoy and appreciate the Lord's blessings and pursue one's calling as guided by the Holy Spirit. Appreciate that you were born in a position to hear the gospel of Christ and receive it. Appreciate that God gave you the faith to believe and understand the gospel message. Appreciate that you have survived childhood and are living an adult life in which you can be a blessing to many others. Appreciate the fact that you may not have any other disability yourself or as a couple other than being unable to bear a child. Look at your husband with new eyes and appreciate that he loves you and his life with you despite being childless. Appreciate that he is not blaming you and has come through his own battle with being childless. Do not shut him out but run this race together to come to the point of embracing your life that God has given you as a couple.

Turn Your Mourning into Dancing for Joy

As I come to a close, I hope I have helped you come to recognize that your experience of infertility and/or childlessness has been experienced by many women. You are not alone. Like me, you have mourned and have walked a path of learning to accept the loss. Your personal experience is unique but there are also many similarities to other infertile, childless women. It has been extremely helpful for me to recognize and become familiar with the experience of other infertile women. What I have shared concerning my experience and what I have learned has, hopefully, helped you not only mourn but move further along in your path to heal and take joy in God's perfect plan for your life.

The time for sadness and mourning is over for me and I hope soon it will be for you, also. Ecclesiastes is often quoted in the section regarding "A Time for Everything" (3:1–8) to comfort those in loss or mourning. However, as written, a "time to mourn," is contrasted with a "time to dance" (Ecclesiastes 3:4). This Scripture emphasizes that there is a time for laughing in contrast to time for weeping. "Weeping may last for the night" but the night is long spent and now, "a shout of joy comes in the morning" (Psalm 30:5b). The morning has arrived. It is time to focus on the joys that can fill one's soul. We may have endured much and will still suffer on this earth but consider what Paul said that this "momentary,

Dancing with Joy to Share

light affliction is producing for us an eternal weight of glory far beyond all comparison" (2 Corinthians 4:17). Joni reminds us, "Our reward will be our joy. The more faithful to God we are in the midst of our pain, the more our reward and joy."[83]

Jesus wants us to experience His joy by abiding in His love, bearing fruit for His kingdom, and following Him in the dance of grace He has given us (John 15:7–10). He said, "These things I have spoken to you, that My joy may be in you, and that your joy may be made full" (John 15:11). "May be made full" is a fantastic concept. How much more can "full" be other than to be so full it is running over? Our lives can be full to running over as we abide in Him, trust Him, and appreciate the life He has given us to love and serve Him. As we give out of our heart of love He has given us by abiding in Him, we will experience love and joy in return. Jesus said, "Give and it will be given to you; good measure, pressed down, shaken together, running over, they will pour into your lap" (Luke 6:38a).

Live in the victory of knowing that God is with you and not against you. He is perfecting you day by day for His glory and for His purpose in your life. He loves you so much that He gave His Son to die and shed His blood to redeem you for Himself and to take away the burden of disappointment that steals your joy. He wants you to be full of the kind of joy

---

83. Joni Eareckson Tada and Steven Estes, *When God Weeps: Why Our Sufferings Matter to the Almighty* (Grand Rapids, MI: Zondervan, 1997), 211.

you can share and not just live for yourself and your personal desires but to bask in His love and share it with others. John Piper said, "Now we see that in creating us for his glory, he is creating us for our highest joy. He is most glorified in us when we are most satisfied in him."[84] Turn your eyes to Him and find that life is not about our disappointments that can turn into bitterness. Life is about living to bring Him the glory due Him. Piper also explains:

> God created us to live with a single passion to joyfully display his supreme excellence in all the spheres of life. The wasted life is the life without this passion. God calls us to pray and think and dream and plan and work not to be made much of, but to make much of him in every part of our lives.[85]

Because of His love through Jesus Christ, God has turned our "mourning into dancing" (Psalm 30:11) for His glory. Do you ever hear a gospel song at home or church that stirs your soul and makes you feel like dancing? Well, join me. Let's get up and dance! Do not hold back any longer. Be glad in the Lord and the way He has made you and designed your life. Like David said, "Let them praise His name with dancing;

---

84. John Piper, *Don't Waste Your Life* (Wheaton, IL: Crossway Books, 2006), 36.
85. John Piper, *Don't Waste Your Life*, 38.

Let them sing praise to Him with timbrel and lyre" (Psalm 149:3).

You are a beautiful woman, designed for a purpose beyond your wildest dreams. Rejoice and be glad! Live your life with exuberance and joy, always moving forward into God's perfection.

BIBLIOGRAPHY

American Pregnancy Association. "Female Infertility: Causes, Treatment and Prevention," American Pregnancy Association. https://www.americanpregnancy.org/infertility/female-infertility/

Boys, John. Exposition of Psalm 113:9. Works of John Boys. Explanatory Notes and Quaint Sayings. Bible Study Tools. http://www.Biblestudytools.com/commentaries/treasury-of-david/psalms-113:9.html.

Bridges, Jerry. *The Pursuit of Holiness*. Colorado Springs, CO: NavPress, 2006.

———. *Trusting God, Even When Life Hurts*. Colorado Springs, CO: NavPress, Tyndale House, 2008.

Briles, Judith, Luci Swindol, and Mary Welchel. *The Workplace: Questions Women Ask*. Portland, OR: Multnomah Books, 1992.

Chanski, Mark. *Womanly Dominion: More Than a Gentle and Quiet Spirit*. Greenville, SC: Calvary Press, 2008.

Cole, Steven J. "Psalm 113: God Is Great and He Is Gracious." Bible.org. https://www.bible.or/seriespage/psalm113-god-great-and-he-gracious.

Davenport, Dawn. "Mental Health of Adoptees." Creating a Family, May 23, 2016. https://creatingafamily.org/adoption-category/mental-health-adoptees/

Devlin, Joseph. *A Dictionary of Synonyms and Antonyms*, Popular Library Edition. New York, NY: Fawcett Popular Library, 1961.

Fuller, Kristen. "Adopted Children More Likely to Develop Mental Health Disorders, Study Shows." Sovereign Health, November 9, 2016. https://www.sovhealth.com/mental-health/adopted-children-likely-develop-mental-health-disorders-study-shows/

George, Elizabeth. *Loving God with All Your Mind*. Eugene, OR: Harvest House Publishers, 1994.

Got Questions Ministries. "What Does the Bible Say about Infertility?" Compelling Truth. https://www.compellingtruth.org/Bible-infertility.html

Grudem, Wayne. *Systematic Theology: An Introduction to Biblical Doctrine*. Grand Rapids, MI: Zondervan, 1994.

Guarino, GinaMarie. "Adopted Children Often Face Mental Health Struggles as Young Adults." Claudia Black Young Adult Center, May 30, 2017. https://www.claudiablackcenter.com/adopted-children-often-face-mental-health-struggles-as-young-adults/

Guthrie, Nancy. *The One Year Book of Hope*. Carol Stream, IL: Tyndale Momentum, 2005.

Henry, Matthew. *Commentary on the Whole Bible in One Volume*, reprint. Grand Rapids, MI: Zondervan Publishing House, 1961.

Jones, Robert D. *Uprooting Anger: Biblical Help for a Common Problem*. Phillipsburg, NJ: P&R Publishing Company, 2005.

BIBLIOGRAPHY

Keener, Craig S. *Miracles: The Credibility of the New Testament Accounts*, 2 vols. Grand Rapids, MI: Baker Academic, 2011.

Kendall, R.T. *The Thorn in the Flesh*. Lake Mary, FL: Charisma House, 2004.

Lewis, C.S. *A Grief Observed*. New York, NY: Bantam Books, 1961.

Lifton, Betty Jean. *Journey of the Adopted Self: A Quest for Wholeness*, New York, NY: Basic Books, 1994. Kindle.

Lowe, Julie Smith. "Counseling the Adopted Child." *The Journal of Biblical Counseling* 25, 3 (Winter 2007). https://www.ccef.org/shop/product/jbc-volume-25-1-pdf/

Ostyn, Mary. *Forever Mom: What to Expect When You're Adopting*. Nashville, TN: Thomas Nelson, 2014. Kindle.

Phillips, J.B. *Your God Is Too Small*. New York, NY: The Macmillan Company, 1961.

Piper, John. *Don't Waste Your Life*. Wheaton, IL: Crossway Books, 2007.

———. *When the Darkness Will Not Lift: Doing What We Can While We Wait for God and Joy*. Wheaton, IL: Crossway Books, 2006.

Reissig, Courtney. "A Barren Woman's Home Is Not Homeless." CBMW.org, March 11, 2015. http://cbmw.wpengine.com/public-square/a-barren-womans-home/.

Saake, Jennifer. *Hannah's Hope: Seeking God's Heart in the Midst of Infertility, Miscarriage and Adoption Loss*. Colorado Springs, CO: NavPress, 2005.

Schmal, Mary. "As God Wills: Understanding God's Plan for Childless Couples." Christian

Life Resources. https://christianliferesources.com/2018/05/08/as-god-wills-understanding-gods-plan-for-childless-couples/

Smith, William. *Smith's Bible Dictionary,* Revised Edition. Nashville, TN: Holman Bible Publishers, 1979.

Spigel, Saul. "Infertility—Causes, Treatment, Insurance and Disability Status." OLR Research Report, February 3, 2005. Connecticut General Assembly. http://www.cga.ct.gov/2005/rpt/2005-R-0145.htm

Stephen, Elizabeth Hervey, and Anjani Chandra. "Updated Projections of Infertility in the United States: 1995–2025." *Fertility and Sterility* 70, 1 (July 1998): 30–34. https://doi.org/10.1016/S0015-0282(98)00103-4

Tada, Joni Eareckson. *A Place of Healing: Wrestling with the Mysteries of Suffering, Pain, and God's Sovereignty.* Colorado Springs, CO: David C. Cook, 2010. Kindle.

———, and Steven Estes. *When God Weeps: Why Our Sufferings Matter to the Almighty.* Grand Rapids, MI: Zondervan, 1997.

Tozer, A.W. *The Knowledge of the Holy: The Attributes of God—Their Meaning in the Christian Life.* New York, NY: Harper & Row, 1961.

US Department of Health & Human Services. "Understanding Fertility: The Basics," OASH | Office of Population Affairs. HHS.gov. http://www.HHS>OPA>ReproductiveHealth>FactsSheets>

Verrier, Nancy N. *The Primal Wound: Understanding the Adopted Child.* San Diego, CA: Nancy Verrier Publications, 1993.

Welch, Edward T. *Depression: A Stubborn Darkness—*

BIBLIOGRAPHY

Light for the Path. Greensboro, NC: New Growth Press, 2004.

Zimmerman, Julie Irwin. *A Spiritual Companion to Infertility.* Skokie, IL: ACTA Publications, 2009.

APPENDIX

Recommended Further Reading

Books

Arbo, Matthew. *Walking through Infertility.* Wheaton, IL: Crossway, 2018.
Baker, Amy. *Infertility, Comfort for Your Empty Arms and Heavy Heart.* Greensboro, NC: New Growth Press, 2013.
Booker, Adriel. *Grace Like Scarlett.* Grand Rapids, MI: Baker Books, 2018.
Bridges, Jerry. *Trusting God.* Colorado Springs, CO: NavPress, 1988.
Curiel, Jessica. *Comfort for Loss* (Pamphlet). Henrickson Publishers, 2011.
George, Elizabeth. *Loving God with All Your Mind.* Eugene, OR: Harvest House, 1994.
Gruelle, Deb. *Aching for a Child,* 2nd Edition. Sacramento, CA: TurquoiseSea Press, 2021.

Guthrie, Nancy. *Hearing Jesus Speak into Your Sorrow.* Carol Stream, IL: Tyndale Momentum, 2009.

———, *What Grieving People Wish You Knew.* Wheaton, IL: Crossway, 2016.

Moreland, J.P. and Scott B. Rae. *Body & Soul: Human Nature & the Crisis in Ethics.* Downers Grove, IL: InterVarsity Press, 2000.

Saake, Jennifer. *Hannah's Hope: Seeking God's Heart in the Midst of Infertility, Miscarriage, and Adoption Loss.* Colorado Springs, CO: NavPress, 2005.

Tada, Joni Eareckson. *A Thankful Heart in a World of Hurt.* Torrance, CA: Aspire Press, Rose Publishing, Inc., 2015.

———, *A Place of Healing: Wrestling with the Mysteries of Suffering, Pain, and God's Sovereignty.* Colorado Springs, CO: David C. Cook, 2010.

———, and Steven Estes. *When God Weeps, Why All Sufferings Matter to the Almighty.* Grand Rapids, MI: Zondervan, 1997.

Tozer, A.W. *The Pursuit of God.* Camp Hill, PA: Christian Publishers, Inc., 1993.

Welch, Edward T. *Depression, Looking Up from the Stubborn Darkness.* Greensboro, NC: New Growth Press, 2011.

Zimmerman, Julie Irwin. *A Spiritual Companion to Infertility.* Skokie, IL: ACTA Publ., 2009.

Books on Adoption

Ayayo, Karelynne Gerber and Michael Ayayo. *Thinking about Adoption.* Eugene, OR: Cascade Books, Imprint of Wipf & Stock Publishers, 2017.

Lifton, Betty Jean. *Journey of the Adopted Self: A Quest*

for Wholeness. New York, NY: Basic Books, 1994.
Newton Verrier, Nancy. *The Primal Wound*. San Diego, CA: Nancy Verrier Publications, December 31, 1993.
Ostyn, Mary. *Forever Mom*. Nashville, TN: Nelson Books, 2014.

Devotionals

Chambers, Oswald. *My Utmost for His Highest*, Updated Edition. Grand Rapids, MI: Discovery House, 1992.
Guthrie, Nancy. *The One Year Book of Hope*. Carol Stream, IL: Tyndale House Publishers, 2005.
Tripp, Paul David. *New Morning Mercies*. Wheaton, IL: Crossway, 2014.

Websites

Care-Net at care-net.org
Heartbeat International at heartbeatinternational.org
Life Perspectives at lifeperspectives.com
Reproductive Loss Network: Connecting Faith, Grief, and Hope at reproductivelossnetwork.org
Saltwater and Honey at saltwaterandhoney.org

www.ingramcontent.com/pod-product-compliance
Lightning Source LLC
Chambersburg PA
CBHW060508100426
42743CB00009B/1259